BUT WILL IT SELL?

ALSO BY MARYA MANNES

MESSAGE FROM A STRANGER

MORE IN ANGER

SUBVERSE

THE NEW YORK I KNOW
Photographs by Herbert Snitzer

But will it sell?

BY MARYA MANNES

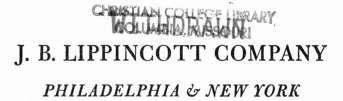

J. B. LIPPINCOTT COMPANY

PHILADELPHIA & NEW YORK

TABLE OF CONTENTS

Contents

BUT WILL IT SELL?

1: Supermarket

PREFACE

IT OCCURS TO ME that this is written largely for the young; more specifically, for the materially comfortable, well-educated young. To those others, deprived of human dignity and the essential rights that sustain it, the first concern is their attainment. The rest—the matters herein discussed—can wait till then. But for you, they cannot.

Some of these pieces are indeed addressed to undergraduates at universities. But most of them, presented in whatever context for whatever reason, are an attempt to hack away at the dense undergrowth of flabby values and rigid attitudes that I believe have been impeding the growth of your elders and may be delaying your own.

Now, people over thirty have either accepted those values and attitudes and will therefore reject with automatic irritation what is said here; or, if they have come independently to conclusions similar to mine, will profit only from the glow of confirmation: a reaction devoutly hoped for by any writer, but in essence passive.

For you, however, these pages might provide ammunition for the kind of rebellion you will have to make if this society of ours is to renew itself. It is an affirmative revolt: not Far Out, which means alienation and abdication, but Far In to the heart of the matter: the path through the woods to the clearing.

For I think this path—call it rut—is choked by a variety of fears which are more imaginary than real and the father of which is change. Change in thinking, change in feeling, change in action.

We have grown old and rich here in America. The old and rich have come to think of our way of life as the only way, and change, to them, means only loss. They resist it with all the massive machinery of their business institutions, their political pressures, and their communications systems. They barricade themselves (and you too) behind this dense thicket as a defense against the winds of change, which is another word for growth.

This is what should worry you more than anything; more than Communism, more than the bomb. For this kind of rigidity and fear is the prelude to the spiritual death that precedes the physical death. It is the hardening of the arteries of society, which marks the withering of that society.

This—the reaction against change which some call conservatism—is the real threat to your future. Don't be misled by golden visions of a simpler life, less government, and more freedom to gain. They have no basis in reality: they lead to isolation from the rest of the world; they are a retreat instead of an advance. They deny the revolution which made us what we are and the revolutions which are changing the world now.

In its extreme forms, conservatism is an attempted return to the past. In its more moderate sense, it is a preservation of the present. And the status quo to which these pages often address themselves, and which the title should make clear, is the invasion of business in areas where it has none.

For this must be the major object of your vigilance now: the government of money—far more powerful and pervasive than the government of laws—which impinges on every sector of your life, affecting not only what you do but how you think and feel. And because it is clothed in the palpable benevolence of prosperity, you accept this impingement, if indeed you are aware of it, as normal and necessary, whether it is the commercials on television, the billboards on highways, or the hideous clutter of your cities. If you think about these at all, you consider them a small price to pay for the strictly private happiness you are free to pursue.

Perhaps you will not think the price quite so small as you read the pages—by no means all solemn—that follow. And if you agree that it may be getting too high, it is time for you, the young consumer-citizen, to question the structure that makes it so and the litany—Give Us This Day Our Daily Profit—that perpetuates it.

THE MONEY THINKERS

"*IT'S PRETTY CRUDE,*" one publisher's reader reported, "and the fellow writes with about as much subtlety as a bulldozer. But it packs enough wallop in the sex scenes to pull in the customers."

"This should support us for the next two years," another wrote, "even though it makes my flesh curl to have us publish it."

13

But Will It Sell?

Said the noted architect to a friend, "I think these new blank-faced apartment houses are a sterile disgrace—boring outside and inside. But what are you going to do when the owners have to get the most return for the least money? Do you think we want to design these deadly boxes?"

As the two drove along the wide main street of a village—more New England than the Eastern Long Island to which it belonged —they passed a corner gas station pressed against the pillared portico of a colonial mansion, half decayed.

"How can they do a thing like that," said the passenger, "to a beautiful old house?"

The driver shrugged. "It's a good corner for business," he said, "and anyhow the old place is a dead loss."

"They were very impressed with your script," said the agent to the young dramatist, "really very enthusiastic about the idea and the writing. But you know how the situation is . . . they just felt the appeal was too special to warrant the cost of production. They can't afford to experiment."

"I'd like to take archeology," said the undergraduate, "but I guess it wouldn't do me much good in a job. . . ."

"Eighty-seven persons were killed in one of the worst air disasters of the year," read the commentator. "We'll bring you the details after this message from Sprinkle, the dandruff remover."

You can go on from there. In every subway the readers of tabloids turn over twelve pages of ads to find one paragraph of news, in city nights stars are blanched by electric sales, and in a million rooms a beer jingle competes for a boy's attention with a problem in math. All these juxtapositions have one thing in common: the impingement of secondary purpose on primary experience.

Or put it another way. If you have ever played a musical

instrument, you'll know what an overtone is. It is any of the higher tones which faintly accompany the fundamental tone produced by the instrument; and it is caused by the vibration of small sections of a string, or an air column.

I was taught at an early age to listen to overtones. My musician parents would bang a tuning fork and hold it to my ear and I would hear the high, almost inaudible after-ping. I haven't thought about it since.

Now it occurs to me that nearly every tone struck today—whether in music or writing or painting or architecture or theatre or anything remotely creative—is accompanied and often distorted by that persistent overtone: But will it sell? It is the shadow that dogs the substance, and it is as tangible as the cloth silhouette that was sewn to the feet of Peter Pan before you were born.

When you hear this overtone or see this shadow, you know, if you have any sense at all, that you are simply being sold something. You put on your consumer's hat and accept the fact that commerce is king and that since the production of goods is the keystone of our national being, the consumption of goods is our national duty.

But soap and cars and clothes and food are one thing. When the fruits of the human mind and spirit become products, then the overtone sours the tone. The measure of worth of a product is quantitative and the measure of worth of a creative act is qualitative, and to apply the standards of the material product to the creative product is to deprive a man, whether he is an artist or not, of his reason for being.

Now I am not saying that art cannot be both good and popular. It can, if the goodness is the result of creative integrity and the popularity a happy consequence of it. It is the initial purpose to appeal to many—to sell to many—that corrupts the primary act.

It may be argued that Americans are so used to this clutter of commerce in their daily lives that we have come to accept it as a necessary, if not always pleasing, corollary to the prosperity of our profit system. It is the realistic price of the real benefits received, among them, we are repeatedly told, a free press, what is called "free" television, and a free society. Any alternative system would, of course, be that most dreadful and dreaded one named (with a hiss of horror) socialism. Indeed this free society is not free to discuss even partial alternatives to the profit system, although some of these alternatives are accepted increasingly in areas where the public good takes precedence over the private advantage. As for the free press and free television, it is surely too much to expect that with their total dependence on advertising revenue they would be free to examine impartially anything that might diminish this revenue. The answer to any criticism of business dominance or interference is invariably: Would you prefer government control? as if government had no business in the affairs of people. Only private enterprise is presumably free to use the public air and the public mind to attain its ends. The citizen has become the consumer, the individual the instrument, not of a super-state, but of the super-market.

At first glance, our kind of brainwashing—for that is what it is—seems infinitely to be preferred. On further inspection, it presents real dangers of its own. For it is a conditioning process that may warp and diminish us in ways less obvious but possibly not much less harmful than the blinkers of state control. Nobody has yet begun to gauge the effect on the mind and spirit of man of the profusion of messages (estimated at 1500 a day) to which he is exposed every day of his life; messages to buy in order to be; the intimate linkage of the product and the person.

Against much of this, to be sure, he has built an immunity, and much of it he does not consciously hear or see. But neither do we consciously sense or see the pollution of the air around us, although it may be infecting our lungs on each intake.

I doubt, moreover, whether the majority of Americans really see the intense ugliness of the visual clutter their cities have become and of the barren stencils their suburban developments are. Nor are they aware that the root of both blights is the victory of the fast buck over the lasting beauty. Here again our environment is shaped not by human need but by business dictation: Take the profit and let the planning go. If neon lights on hot-dog stands pull the customers in, to hell with the look of the street. If you can sell fifty houses instead of thirty on a twenty-acre tract, to hell with trees, space, architectural variety, and individual privacy. In the race for money, some men may come first, but man comes last.

Conversely, the best planning and the finest design are lavished on office buildings. These are the temples of the official religion. For once the tone and the overtone are consonant: the fulfillment, through buying and selling, of a nation's material needs.

But it is the needs of the single mind that concern us here. There is just so much inner space in each man, and what fills it is the measure of the man; the extent to which, beyond the daily concerns, he can address himself to the grand questions of life and death, of love and creation. If this miraculous inner space becomes—through cumulative and incessant exposure to what is trivial, superfluous, and irrelevant—as cluttered as the aisles of the supermarket, it ends by losing its primary function as the sanctuary of conscience and the seat of thought. The man who is the victim of things is neither free nor excellent. Living more and more by the priorities of possessions, position, and purse, he does not see beyond them. The overtone is drowning out the tone; or, let us say, the overtone has replaced the tone.

If this is so—and I would not be writing it if I did not think it was—how can we begin to alter the balance of the mind so that the overtone becomes not "will it sell?" but "is it good?" How can we protect the inner sanctuary of conscience and creation from the intruders who come between the search and the truth?

In small ways, the process has already begun. To their profound concern, advertisers are noticing a growing indifference among the mass of television viewers to what they are selling. The consumer is so sated with messages that many of them now fail to register. More than that, the relentless intrusion of sales into what is supposed to be entertainment and information is forcing government, at last, to attempt some limitation of commercial time on the air.

Noncommercial educational television is gaining more and more outlets and, in spite of major difficulties in acquiring financial backing and sufficient talent, attracting more and more people who want to be told instead of sold, to be stimulated rather than distracted, to learn rather than lounge.

Listener-supported FM radio stations are on the increase, in spite of the kind of harassment that recently threatened to silence Pacifica, permitting the public access to a range of thought and opinion denied them on most commercial radio, to a wealth of music and literature, to satire and criticism. And no sales.

Alternatives to the commercial theatre—strangled by pressures from theatre owners, craft unions, and talent agencies who have nothing to do with the creative act—are now proliferating throughout the country: in university play groups, in professional actors' groups, in neighborhood theatre societies open to experiment rather than profit.

Brave individuals have been telling Americans what is being done to them without their knowledge: the exploitation of bereavement by the funeral merchants, the destruction of our natural environment by the chemical polluters, the exploitation of our fears and illnesses by the drug marketers.

And there are still publishers of books and papers and magazines who put truth above expedience and the reader's needs ahead of the seller's market.

It is such arts and such people who must be supported if any balance is to be restored between the temporal and the spiritual, between commerce and communion, between gain and good. I would even like to see the beginning of a deliberate restraint: not the denial of those basic comforts which our system has so successfully produced for so many, but the recognition of a point at which consumption has become a habit instead of a need and is therefore harmful.

This is heresy in a society which has so far prospered by the encouragement of unlimited consumption, but I hold to it. And if the point at which each of us says No is hard to define, it is still recognizable to the honest: the moment when we begin to confuse what we are with what we have; when we think we need what we do not need; and when, in order to satisfy these illusory needs, we sell ourselves.

It was to pin this recognition down that much of this book was written. But will it sell? Probably not. The price of attacking business is to lose business.

But then, I am not talking to the sellers. I am talking to the sold.

MAGAZINE OR MARKET

ARE YOU READING MORE and enjoying it less?

Do you like following a column of text through thirty pages of ads?

Can you find the articles in a Sunday newspaper magazine with sixty pages of clothes?

Are you annoyed by having to leaf through twenty pages of sales to find your columnist?

Or have you taken this all for granted as a means towards an end: a free press?

As one who has not, I have conducted a small survey of my own as to how far you can mix business (selling) with pleasure (reading) without ultimately harming both, and how much the sustained confusion of sights and messages may have become also a confusion of values that is in the end corrupting. It is a question which our mass magazines in particular had better ask themselves and which this particular reader suspects is at the root of their troubles. In their ferocious competition for advertising space, they may find themselves gaining revenue but losing readers. Can you be equally magazine and market, or is there a point at which the market is more than the magazine?

In an attempt to find out for myself, I decided to examine *Life,* not because it was unique—the big women's magazines, *Look,* the *Saturday Evening Post,* even the *New Yorker* share many of its attributes—but because it seemed to typify more clearly than these the steady deterioration in reader interest brought about by the quantity and quality of advertising.

I started this examination with an issue that appeared during the first year of *Life's* existence, on January 4, 1937. It contained sixty-eight pages, of which fifty-nine were editorial. The body of the magazine consisted of forty-nine editorial pages without any advertising whatsoever, the subjects being the Netherlands royal family, sports, racing, the Metropolitan Opera opening, the Roosevelt administration (sixteen pages), Maillol, the Camera Overseas, Ribbentrop, the French and Germans, the Cubans, and the Danes.

It was a strange, long-forgotten experience to turn over page after page, uninterrupted by extraneous matter, of photographs and captions. The pictures looked gray and showed little of the technical brilliance and dramatic selection that characterize the best of *Life* photography, the layouts were unadventurous by current standards; yet it was not hard to remember the excitement then engendered by this new form—like an arrested movie —of journalism. What emerged with startling clarity, moreover, was that this was a magazine and not a market. What was solicited was the reader's interest in a story or event, and nothing was presented to distract his attention from them, except, I remember noting, one full-page ad for a Plymouth at the front of the issue, a half-page for Del Monte canned fruit, and a *Time* house ad at the back. By the end of 1937, *Life* had a circulation of 1,384,000 and an advertising revenue of some $4.4 million. Twenty-four years later, by the end of 1961, *Life's* circulation had risen to nearly seven million copies, its advertising revenue to over $138 million. The formula that originated this revolution in publishing would have seemed, therefore, to work. Yet it has not worked for me.

In the issue of May 25, 1962, for instance, five two-page spreads are devoted to a feature on the private papers, recently released, of one of this nation's most illustrious men, John Adams. Illustrated by superb color photographs and small black-and-white prints in a layout of dignity and balance, it is a prime example of the best in pictorial journalism, feeding both the eye and the mind, making past and present alive.

Following these two-page spreads is a single-page color photograph, magnificent in sunlit tones and tranquil mood, of the chair in Adams's study where he is said to have died. This page faces a huge ad in primary colors of a grinning young couple holding a bottle, a golf club, and a golf score, the copy reading, "Now it's Pepsi—for those who *think young*." Turning this over, a full page of Adams in text with one small print faces a full-page ad in violent red and yellow: "Buick Introduces Torrid New Luxury Sports Car! First with the Sure-Footed Sock of Advanced Thrust!" Next comes a black-and-white two-page spread about how "you live better electrically." Further on, two columns of Adams text, including paragraphs grouped under a subhead "The Fourth of July" (the Golden Jubilee, in 1826, of the signing of the Declaration of Independence and the day that both Adams and Jefferson died), are faced with a full-page bleed photograph of a contemporary Fourth of July small-town scene, uniformed school band and all. It looks editorial but a line at the bottom discloses it as a Polaroid Camera ad.

At one point in the feature there are two broad columns of text in which the old Adams writes the old Jefferson, "You and I ought not to die, before we have explained ourselves to each

But Will It Sell?

other." His words are flanked on either side by two huge male walking feet in shoes and socks (by Esquire). The caption of the left foot (formal sock and shoe) is "Don't mix business . . . ," and the caption of the right foot (casual sock and loafer) is "with pleasure." As far as I am concerned, no single juxtaposition of editorial and advertising matter could indicate more clearly, in word and picture, how much business has indeed mixed with pleasure even if it is only my pleasure.

For I find the *Life* of 1937, when the ratio of advertising to editorial matter was six per cent, infinitely more interesting and enjoyable than the *Life* of 1963, when the ratio is fifty per cent. The years between have seen a steady diminution of purely editorial spreads, an increased interruption of editorial matter by two-page-spread ads, and a much greater increase of editorial text as an accommodation for advertising matter. Two decades ago, *Life* told its stories in pictures; now text is a full partner.

Since the amount of advertising in a publication is a measure of the breadth of its editorial appeal, this increase alone should present no problem to readers long conditioned to this fact of life in a free and competitive economy. They might have a little more trouble finding their favorite features or following a specific story, they might grumble at the increased bulk, but so long as the separation of telling and selling was clear, so long as the advertising did not compete with, affect, or impinge upon the editorial matter, this equal sharing of space was—well—an index of success.

But were the two really separated? To those who think of influence only as the direct interference of advertising interests in editorial policy or copy, the answer would be yes. Provable instances in reputable magazines of advertisers telling editors what to put in or take out, how to handle a story or temper an attitude, are rare, although cases of omission—not printing a story because it might lose certain accounts—may be more frequent even though less provable. What we are treating of here is rather the effect of quantity advertising on the quality of a magazine, on its physical appearance, and on the attention and interest of the readers.

There are two major ways in which advertising does impinge on and affect editorial material: at the one extreme it is difficult at first glance to tell what is a feature and what is an ad; at the other, incongruous advertising is jarringly juxtaposed with editorial matter.

Cases of confusing similarity between editorial material and advertising layouts were already to be found in *Life* in 1942. In the January 5 issue of that year there was an example typical of what later became a widespread practice in its pages. A two-page spread using editorial phototechniques, layout, and type was titled "Behind the Scenes in a Huge Bomber Plant." The captions informed us that it was Glenn Martin, but it was not until the end that the reader in search of a story found instead a plug for the Voicewriter Ediphone used in the plant—and paying for these pages.

The confusion worked the other way around too. You saw a full-page photograph, say, of a family at dinner, and although the caption concerned the life of a Midwestern farmer, you looked instinctively for the brand name of a food product.

If this kind of confusion has lessened in recent years, it is not so much because of an indignant readership or editorial resistance as the switch to a harder sell. The way to get a reader was not to lure him gently by making the transition from reader to consumer so muted as to be painless; it was to hit him between the eyes. To play strong color against black-and-white, type brazenly different from editorial type—this was, and is, the new way: contrast rather than confusion. It could be, and doubtless has been, argued that this is the "ethical" way: to keep advertising and editorial unmistakably different and therefore separate. But what has actually happened in the picture magazines and in *Life* especially is that such violent juxtapositions often hurt the editorial side by reducing the impact of the photograph, diminishing the meaning of the text by incongruous context, and by sheer visual ugliness nibbling away at the reader's pleasure in the

magazine as a whole. It is a further irony that the more brilliant
and sometimes beautiful the pictures by the *Life* photographers
become, the more the blatant and primitive commercialism of
the ads harms or nullifies their efforts.

Look with me at another issue, for instance. These things
face each other: the text of the trial and conviction of Raoul
Salan, with all its shame, tension, and horror, is opposed by a
full-page color photograph for Newport cigarettes showing a
beaming pair on a rock in a blue lake on which a king-size pack
floats by. It is a loud, garish, and silly ad from which the eye
cannot escape. Further on, a piece on Ambassador Reischauer
in Japan is squeezed in an eight-page ad-plus-editorial layout
of unparalleled ugliness. At the top of one page four Zengakuren
students, their features stretched in hostility, are chanting protests against the resumption of U.S. nuclear tests. Directly below
them is the inevitably grinning All-American young man holding
up a dozen cans of Budweiser beer against a bright orange background and urging the reader to Pick a Pair. This one-page
jumble is in turn faced by a full-page ad for Scripto pens. On
the following two pages, our ambassador to the Japanese ("I
have to approach [Japanese students] as a scholar, not just as a
mouthpiece for the American position") has to compete in face
and in words with another orange Budweiser pitch (this time
by a girl) and a full-page Chevrolet ad. The whole thing con-
stitutes some kind of American "position" that he might have
some difficulty explaining in scholarly terms.

In other random issues during the last ten years we have Isaac
Stern and Leonard Bernstein wedged between Borden's cow Elsie
and a little girl using a Sylvania iron; a full-page Tareyton color
ad facing the crash of a DC 8 jet; and a photograph of Pasternak's
funeral, with his beloved Olga kissing the poet's dead brow,
facing an ad for the Commercial Banks, U.S., in which a fellow
is hamming in amateur theatricals. A magnificent full-page photograph of Etruscan tomb figures faces a cola-and-rum ad; a subtle
and lovely Degaslike color photograph of a ballet is nullified by

Supermarket

a full-page bowl of tomato soup. James Agee is sandwiched between Falling Hair, Tums, and Choco Cherry Spumoni; Sir Charles Snow is squeezed between constipation and valentines, Professor Tizard between colored fruits and glue. Hurricane waves lashing at a Texas tower, which they ultimately destroyed along with its crew, compete for attention with a smiling full-page goddess in Formfit girdle and bra.

Again, these grotesque distractions are not confined to *Life*. *Look*, its closest rival, is sometimes as much of a hodgepodge, a supermarket in which a shelf of information, news, or sports is alternated with soups, dog food, cars, cigarettes, and beer. In a recent issue a page of serious text on children's education faces a girl dreaming she stopped them in their tracks in her Maidenform Bra (and red fringed pants); and another page, headed "A child will learn better the more often he is right," faces "Is it true . . . blondes have more fun?" with loving couples in living color. The opening spread of this feature seems a particularly unfortunate juxtaposition: over the inch-high type "Revolution in Education," a close-up of a boy's face peers over the top of a teaching machine at a huge platter of hamburgers glowing redly in Kraft Barbecue Sauce. What is more, only forty-four of *Look's* hundred pages are devoted purely to editorial matter, a very small percentage higher than *Life's* fifty-seven to 110. So why pick on *Life* in this question of confusion of values, of business at the expense of pleasure?

The answer lies, I think, in another kind of juxtaposition, a very basic one: between promise and performance, purpose and effect. If *Look* has a purpose other than to attract a wide range of lookers, it is carefully concealed from view. But *Life* has always had an Aim, which it has defined periodically since it was launched. Then it was "To see life; to see the world; to eyewitness great events; to watch the faces of the poor and the gestures of the proud . . . to see and take pleasure in seeing; to see and to be instructed." "The Show-Book of the World"—for that is what it called itself in its original prospectus—"takes for its field not all the news but all the news which now and hereafter can be seen; and *of these seen events it proposes to be the complete and reliable record."* It promises also "to scour the world for the best pictures of every kind; to edit them with a feeling for visual form, for history and for drama; and to publish them on fine paper, every week, for a dime." Instruction, documentation, distinguished graphic innovation—these were the early goals; immediate news and lasting significance in pictorial terms for an audience assumed to be as intelligent as it was large. As time went on, more and more readers were taught more and more things. In between fraternity parties, sexy starlets, and play-clothes, they learned the Epic of Man, the History of Art, the Civil War, the nature of the Land, the Sea, and the Universe, all in color with brisk and knowing text that made such things assimilable in two issues if not in one. Besides giving its readers such quantities of facts, *Life* taught them how to think, how to react, and how to vote, handing down a steady barrage of editorial counsel on political matters, national and international, and on cultural and moral problems of the day. In a recent issue, facing five different Snow Crop oranges ("This is Seedling. The bubbly type, with a bright sweet spirit"), the editorial says, "It's High Time to Blow the Whistle on Tito" and "We Must Act Now for Refugees [Chinese]."

Now there is nothing wrong with a magazine wishing to improve its readers, or, for that matter, the world. Not long ago, *Life's* publisher, C. D. Jackson, set forth a refurbished and even more comprehensive purpose called "The Aim of *Life."* After describing the changes that had occurred in the magazine's format —"You may also be aware of new groupings of the editorial and advertising pages to give more clarity to the pattern of the magazine, more space to *Life's* major stories"—he wrote, "We seek to strengthen *Life's* graphic presentation for one simple reason: we believe *Life* has increasingly important work to do."

This work, it turns out, is to (1) Win the Cold War and (2) Create a Better America. "Can a magazine presume to say it will

Supermarket

help win the Cold War, help create a better America? I cannot presume otherwise." Presuming further that *Life* was already bringing "beauty and knowledge and understanding to receptive millions of Americans," Mr. Jackson stated that in the next twenty-five years the aim of *Life* was to be a great magazine of Events and Politics, a great magazine of History, a great magazine of Religion, a great magazine of Science and Nature, a great magazine of the Fine and Lively Arts, a great magazine of Sport and Adventure, a great magazine of Better Living . . . to help "the people of America recognize their deepest aspirations and work unceasingly towards fulfillment."

A noble program indeed. But is it compatible with an uncontrolled proliferation of advertising to the tune of $138,189,000 a year? Can a magazine have its cake and eat it too? Down the aisles of the supermarket—the soups, the cars, the dog food, the bras, the cigarettes, the beers, and the wienies—*Life* pushes its cart of Moral and Spiritual Values, nudging its customers to lift their eyes to the hills while they reach for a Pepsi. As *Life* initiates them into the majesties of Rembrandt and the immortal attributes of art and beauty, it subjects them to a graphic nightmare of crass layouts, of a blaring and brazen carnival of sales. As it urges Americans to think, to discriminate, to improve, as it appeals to the national intelligence, it permits this same intelligence to be abused week after week and page after page by banal and blatant appeals to the purse. As it claims to "strengthen *Life's* graphic presentation"—and it did indeed make a vain attempt in recent months to keep "islands" of editorial matter intact—it still seems unable to stem an ever-increasing encroachment of advertising matter that makes the magazine, in fact, a graphic mess.

Again, the basic confusion of magazine with market is not confined to *Life* or even to picture magazines in general. The *New Yorker,* long noted for its independence from advertising pressures or incursions, has lost some of its most faithful adherents because the sheer bulk of advertising matter has caused the text of single articles to trickle down as many as thirty pages in thin and seemingly endless columns in the back of the magazine. Many an excellent story has gone unread for this reason only. For it is the good that suffers most. A profusion of ads, even ugly ads, cannot harm mediocre or trivial text any more than a tasteless television commercial harms a silly situation comedy. It is the fine photograph, the serious or subtle word, that is harmed by juxtaposition with the sales pitch. And it is the stated high purpose, the presumption of a magazine to educate its readers, that makes its truckling to the advertisers open to the sharpest questioning. If the supermarket is the victor, the reader is the victim. And once he is aware of that, the mass magazine is in trouble.

A WORD TO THE WIZARDS

ASKING ME TO ADDRESS a conference of advertisers is a little like having a rabbit address a Planned Parenthood Meeting. To put it gently, you and I don't always see things the same way. I keep shouting for a higher standard of thinking instead of a higher standard of living, and I keep accusing you people of making us people want a lot of things we don't need and buy a lot of things we can't afford.

Yet although I may not have thought of advertising as the

single greatest contribution to human welfare, I do know what it has done for us. It has made us look good, smell good, and live good—like a citizen should. Advertising does great because the agencies are. What's more, advertising does not—contrary to some detractors—concern itself only with material values. I understand that in the Middlewest the Presbyterian Church ran a test campaign to find out whether advertising could interest more people in religion. Apparently Stan Freberg wrote the jingles, one of which contains the uplifting line: "Doesn't it get a little lonely sometimes—out on that limb without Him?"

Inspired by this, I've made up a few jingles myself.

Try Prayer—it purifies the air.

Take Belief—for fast, fast, *fast* Relief.

Or what about this: Left in the lurch? No help from Birch? Try Church. And now, the weather. . . .

To be—with some difficulty—serious, the question I'm supposed to kick around here is, How Well do Advertisers Know the Consuming Public? Considering the volume of sales that makes this country the most prosperous in the world, the answer should be obvious: They know us very well. Heaven knows, the American consumer has for years been the object of an unrelenting scrutiny that measures everything from his salary to his saliva, from his pulse to his purse, from his libido to his liver. Now they've got a secret eye camera that checks up on your pupil dilations. A fellow looks at a package of Fig Newtons, say, and if he likes Fig Newtons, his pupils dilate, and if he doesn't, they contract. The marketing people say this little camera is much more reliable than the consumer, who, presumably, is a natural born liar. They mention the case of a man who said he preferred a business magazine article to a racier item in a man's magazine, but when he was shown the racier item—I wonder what that could have been?—his eyes dilated. I guess this proved that he liked nudes better than news. It's marvelous what science is doing.

Anyway, with or without these peeping-tom techniques, advertisers do know a lot of basic things about us people. They know that women like to be thin but would rather eat cream-fudge layer cake. They know that men want to look virile but would rather be comfortable. They know that people want dry beer instead of wet beer. They know that children want every-thing—and get it.

But there are an amazing number of things they don't know. Things they don't need to be told by secret cameras or personality tests, by poll or survey. Things that ordinary observation of daily life should tell them. Things that an elementary understanding of human nature should make clear.

I'd like to start with some examples, and if they apply to television rather than to print, it is partly because advertising on TV reaches the greatest number of consumers and has therefore the widest over-all impact, and partly because I think that television advertising lags considerably behind printed advertising in its assessment of, and appeal to, the consumer.

Take this hair-tint commercial, for instance. There's this row of suburban homes, and you see two wives waiting in their neighboring doorways to greet two commuting husbands back from a tough day in the city and three bar-car martinis.

Well, we close in on one of the wives, and she's a very pretty woman indeed with an interesting streak in her hair and a sweet smile on her face. The husband of the other woman walks by with a bunch of flowers for *his* mate, but *her* husband is empty handed. Her smile vanishes as she thinks out loud: Is it my grey streak? Her tragic face fades out. We see her next having washed her grey away and become a varnished brunette dressed to the teeth and arranging roses in a vase. Enter husband in dinner jacket and leer. Wife sticks one rose in husband's lapel, husband takes it out and sticks it in his teeth. They do a revolting little dance together, he wraps her in mink, and they waltz off to a night on the town. Now everything in this little concoction is the sheerest nonsense, and every viewer knows it. Men do not neglect their wives because they have a grey streak. (There are fifty better reasons.) Men do not stick roses in their teeth after a hard day at the office. Men very rarely bring flowers back on

Supermarket

the six-ten anyway, even to blondes. But there's something much worse than that here: a distortion of values that will make women worry about the wrong things in life. There are a hundred ways of selling hair tint without making love depend on it. And advertisers in general bear a large part of the responsibility for the deep feelings of inadequacy that drive women to psychiatrists, pills, or the bottle. You keep telling us over and over that if only we would use that or have this or look like that, we would be forever desirable, forever happy. So we spend our time worrying over the grey streak or the extra pound or the dry skin instead of our minds, our hearts, and our fellow men.

Now back to the little screen for further evidence of advertiser ignorance of the consumer. They don't know children. Children do not come rushing home to their parents shouting "Mom, our group had twenty per cent less cavities than the others!" Little boys do not know the difference between scratchy towels and soft towels because they seldom use them. Big boys don't either. In fact, big boys, or men, do not notice when their shirts are whiter. They don't notice laundry at all unless their buttons are torn off. The whole subject of wash and detergents is a big yawning bore to the male, and any female dumb enough to bring her new bleaches into the conversation will not latch onto him long.

But the real area of stupefying advertiser ignorance of the consumer is the biggest one of all: women. They are, of course, the prime targets, because they are the prime buyers. And gentlemen, if I may call you that, you don't know us at all.

For one thing, out of the nearly forty-three million wives in this country, over fourteen million of us work. But you, the advertisers, continue to assume that all American women are housewives only, bound in perpetuity to sink, stove, and nursery. I have yet to see an ad or commercial in which the woman involved buys a product because it helps her speed up her chores after a working day. I have yet to see any reference to or any mention of the fact that these fourteen million women who have jobs need certain products even more than *their* home-bound and time-free sisters. There is in advertising no recognition of this major social and economic fact: that more and more women have jobs as well as homes and that they constitute a huge, enlightened, and demanding consumer group which should be recognized, and appealed to, as such.

For another thing, over one hundred forty thousand women are college alumnae, and many million are high school graduates —and presumably educated. But I have yet to see a commercial in which a woman lays down a book or leaves a piano or interrupts her needlepoint in order to get on with some household chore. Nor, for that matter, have I seen any woman in a commercial with an IQ over 95. According to advertisers, women are a garrulous, scatterbrained bunch of suckers who have nothing to do but polish and cook, and nothing to talk about but soap and food.

Is this a true image of the American woman? And if it isn't, are you deliberately trying to make it so in order to sell more products? If you are, you are doing not only us but the nation a disservice. For I don't think the advertisers have any real idea of their power not only to reflect, but to mold, society. And if you reflect us incorrectly, as I believe you are doing, you are raising a generation of children with cockeyed values as to what men and women and life and family really are. You may be training them as consumers, but you are certainly not educating them as people.

And don't say that your job is to sell and not educate. I have the word of Hugh Downs himself, in a recent speech, in which he says that "the promotion of a good product is a form of education and a form that serves truth in the same way as promotion of an ethical ideal."

Are you serving truth, for instance, when not one of the nineteen million Negroes in this country is shown on television as a consumer of products? Don't colored housewives have laundry, wash diapers, wax floors, bake layer cake? Don't colored girls want to look beautiful? Don't Negroes buy beer? Is there any good reason why men might not vote for a lovely dark Miss Rheingold?

Supermarket

But still, in all your advertising, you—or I really should say the sponsors—persist in showing a white middle-class suburban world of two-car garages, white-collar husbands, and aproned women, when the real, turbulent, fascinating, pluralistic world that is America tells a vastly different story.

And what about that very hot potato, cigarette advertising? Some of you, for obvious reasons and millions of dollars, still refuse to admit that the link between smoking and cancer, which the highest scientific bodies in several countries have officially established, does indeed exist. You go right on television, at hours when children are looking, showing young, handsome people puffing away as if smoking was the normal, healthy, romantic way of life. It goes with status and love and youth and pretty country and all pleasant things. So naturally, the minute a kid is fourteen he wants to smoke too.

Now, I have noticed that one advertiser is trying to make his male smokers, on TV and in print, the mature types (what is the slogan—separating the men from the boys?) in the naive belief that only adults will be encouraged to indulge. But don't all boys want to ape grown men—in clothes, in cars, in talk—and certainly in habits? Do you really think that this kind of pitch is going to escape them?

Now, everybody knows that millions of adults like to smoke and have no intention of stopping for any reason. Certainly, cigarette manufacturers have every intention of continuing to cater to this popular human indulgence, whatever its hazards. But the hazards are real, the danger is there, and it would seem to me that the advertiser who cares about his consumer would devise some means of letting him know this.

I am not naive enough to think that cigarette advertising will, or should, cease. But I am interested enough in the fate of my fellow Americans to suggest that advertisers seriously consider new approaches to selling their highly controversial product. In England, for instance, cigarette advertising on TV is confined to late evening hours when children are presumably not viewing. But there are other approaches too. Would not this kind of slogan get the right message across: A Habit is Not a Pleasure: Don't

But Will It Sell?

Smoke Because You Have to—Smoke Because You Want to. Surely the theme of moderation is the answer: Don't Be Hooked —Be Healthy. Smoke Less and Enjoy It More. . . .

But again, seriously, my quarrel with advertisers is really this: that they do not realize the power they have. And I don't mean the power to move goods. I don't even mean the power, which they have exercised to their credit and the nation's economy, to raise the standard of living in this country beyond anything man has yet seen. The power I mean is the power to affect, deeply and lastingly, the nature, attitudes, and aspirations of a hundred and eighty million Americans. For years advertisers have been conditioning us not just to buy certain things but to live and think and aspire in certain ways.

On the material level, these ways have been largely good. On the human or spiritual or moral level, I am not at all sure they are. And I do not mean here the problem of misleading or deceptive advertising: on the whole, most products perform as they are claimed to do; for if they didn't, people would stop buying them. No, I am referring to a misleading and deceptive view of life and people that could, in the long run, be detrimental to American society. For it is not enough to show people how to *live* better: there is a mandate for any group with enormous powers of communication to show people how to *be* better. The two are not incompatible, but they can be divorced and they are being divorced by the foolish images of American home life that we see day in and day out on the TV screen or on the pages of magazines.

And in this connection, I would like to point out what one form of advertising is doing to the nation's children and their relationships to their parents. In the last years (and I am quoting a *New York Times* article) researchers have found that ninety-four per cent of mothers interviewed said their children demanded that they buy certain items they had seen advertised on television. Great, you say, what a market: forty million children becoming consumers from the age of three onward!

But it's not great. It's creating a race of demanding, nagging, overindulged, overpampered kids—and a race of beaten-down, spineless parents who take their orders. Even the advertisers are beginning to see this. One man, Mr. Charles Goldschmidt, the Chairman of an agency, said "I think some advertisers are trying too hard to appease the kids."

How right he is. And what a major disservice this kind of appeasement is to any decent sense of values. You, the advertisers, have a mandate to teach values of more than your product. Infinitely more people get your messages than read the editorial contents of magazines or look—and I mean really look—at most television programs. They may think they watch the programs, but what stays with them are the unending interruptions: the commercial kiddies who whine for fried chicken when their mother has cooked them something else, the half-witted housewife who doesn't know she's on camera, the irritable man who has acid indigestion, the miserable man who can't breathe, the saccharine mothers and daughters who look alike (but I bet don't think alike), the overdressed young lovers who smoke by waterfalls, . . . You name it, we get it. And it's a wholesale perversion of reality.

Oh, sometimes it isn't. Whoever thought up the small boy who prefers Oreos to little girls was on the right track. And so was the fellow who showed little kids viewing the new baby in the family with considerable distaste. Some of you advertisers—and many in the print media—have kept your eyes and ears open and sold your product in a real world to real people. You are the ones with respect for your fellow Americans as well as for your product, and you are to be saluted. You are also lucky in your enlightened clients. For in the last analysis, it is the sponsor and not the advertiser who is the real culprit in the manufacture of this advertising dream world of false values.

For advertisers as a whole are a lively, observant, sophisticated lot who, left to themselves, would probably not produce the nonsense they do. But let's face it: they need the accounts more than they need my approval, or even the gratitude of millions of consumers who have suffered the serious stereotypes and endless repetitions of so many of their commercials.

So, you see, I am really very pro-advertisers. All I want is that they cast the scales off their eyes, see the world as it is, and sell honesty to the sponsor as the best way not only to move his product but to benefit the health, education, and welfare of an entire nation. They have the power, and the obligation, to do so.

But they can't do it until they take a new, long, hard, fresh look at us—the consumers—so that we can recognize ourselves as we really are.

PACKAGED DECEPTION

NOTE: What follows was testimony given to the Subcommittee on Antitrust and Monopoly in Washington, D. C., three years ago. Since then, business resistance to proposed and pending legislation has been monumental. But the publicity attending the investigations and the mounting consumer outcry have already resulted in much clearer designations of weights and prices on the packages of several major manufacturers. The threat of legislation is achieving some of the aims of legislation: another proof of the power of single voices—combined.

I AM A WRITER and a housewife. As a writer I sell words and ideas. They are not packaged. The buyer can see exactly what they are and pay what he thinks they are worth. As a housewife I buy what is sold to me. It is packaged. I buy it on faith. That is why, these days, the word consumer is sometimes spelled s-u-c-k-e-r.

And that is why I stand before you here not as a writer but as a sucker, one of millions who wonder why so much money drains out of the foodbag and the handbag every week, and who then forget about it.

Now, I have always believed that the majority of people were too good to be smart. Ever since we bartered a beaver pelt for ten eggs, we have assumed that the eggs were fresh and the pelt was supple, for how else can decent business be transacted? Except for the relation between man and wife, nothing is more intimate than the relation between the buyer and the seller; and there would be neither marriage nor commerce if the fundamental basis of both were not trust. Without trust, a civilized society cannot endure. When the people who are too smart to be good fool the people who are too good to be smart, then society begins to crumble. I think this is what is happening now, and I believe it must be stopped before our integrity as Americans is chiseled away as fast as our dollars are.

What am I talking about? I am talking about certain practices in the market which manage to evade the spirit of the law while adhering by an eyelash to the letter of the law. I am talking about what happens when a housewife like myself goes to buy food for her family, and how she spends her money doing it.

And I am talking about the many small deceptions, most of them deliberate, which make a rational buying choice—the basis of free enterprise—meaningless. You can only choose when you know what you are choosing, and the plain truth is that much of the time we don't. That great American institution, the supermarkets, those gleaming palaces of convenience and bounty, have come to be the greatest exercise in planned confusion since the bazaars of Samarkand. If you don't believe me, climb into my pushcart and come around with me, shelf by shelf.

Need some applesauce for the baby? Pick up a few of Brand A's new jars. They look just like the old ones. They cost the same. But do you know that the new jar has only seven and a half ounces of applesauce while the old one had seven and three-quarters ounces? No? You mean you didn't *look* at that fine print with your glasses? Now, how about some breakfast food? Well, Brand B's old box contained six biscuits and weighed six ounces, but when you open the new box which is exactly the same size, you'll find only five ounces of biscuits—a drop in contents of about sixteen per cent. Oh sure, they tell you what's inside the jar or box, but you need a slide rule to figure out the difference. And what housewife with a kid inside the cart and one at her heels can spare the time?

This is confusion number one: to make you think you're getting the same value in the same box at the same price when you're actually getting less. If you complain, the manufacturers say that they're saving you a price raise by reducing the contents. Can you beat it?

Confusion number two is in sizes. Know the difference between Giant and Jumbo? Between two-ounce and a *big* two-ounce? Between a quart and a *full* quart? What's a *tall* 24-inch? What does Extra Long mean? Who's kidding who? And what's the matter with simple sizes, like a pint or two pints or a quart or two quarts? I'll tell you what's the matter. They're too easy to figure. You might know what you were getting. And that goes for the Economy Size too. What economy? If you stop to figure it out, half the time the price per unit remains exactly the same regardless of size, and you save nothing. It just seems economic to us suckers.

Now, let's stop at detergents, where the Giant sizes are. Well, with a box of Brand C, *Giant* means three pounds, five and one-half ounces, but with Brand D, *Giant* means three pounds one and one-fourth ounces; but both boxes look the same size and cost the same price—77 cents. Are the ingredients of the one so superior to the ingredients in the other that four ounces don't matter? And how do you know it, anyway?

Let's move next door to the All-Purpose liquid cleaners. With 69 cents you can buy one quart of Brand E, or 1 pint, 12 fluid ounces of Brand F. The shapes are slightly different, but they look the same size. Do you know where the four ounces go? Do you care?

Want some soap pads? Well, you can buy a box of Brand G or a box of Brand H for 13 cents, but unless you turn the box upside down and use your bifocals, you won't know that there are only four pads of Brand G compared to five pads of Brand H. Care about one less pad? Half the time, the quantity of such products is printed in very small type or in a color that merges in the background. Sometimes it's even printed *underneath* the flap, and you can't see it until you open it. Do you see it even then?

Now, you would think that if packages were different sizes, they'd contain different amounts, but that's because you're congenitally dumb. Brand I, a table salt, is in a box one inch taller than Brand J, another table salt, but each has exactly one pound and ten ounces in them. And how are you to know if the first box is slightly thinner than the second one? Where was your tape measure?

Then there are the simple devices of not really filling the box or bottle. You open up a cereal, say, and you find an inch or more space on the top—slack-filled, it's called. Or the liquid in a bottle has an inch or more empty space above it. And there's the business of using paper to wrap around crackers or soap and fill the loose space. The manufacturers will, of course, claim these are necessary for safe handling and so forth. But we're paying enough for outer space not to have to pay for inner space, too.

There's another good gimmick to confuse you: funny shapes of bottles that make any real estimate of contents impossible.

Then there are all those lovely phrases like the New, the Improved, the Activated, the Super, and so forth. Don't they give you the impression that you are getting a better product, justifying a higher price? Well, half the time you aren't. These words are like the bells the scientists ring to make dogs salivate. You see the word "new" and you reach for it.

For now, you see, there is no salesman any more to tell you what you are getting. In supermarkets, the *package* is the salesman. The more space he takes up on the shelf (*that's* the reason for Giant and Jumbo, *not* economy), the louder his letters scream at you, the sooner you'll notice him. But while he shouts "Buy me!" he also talks double-talk out of the side of his mouth. And while you put *him* in your cart, he picks *your* pocket.

Why? Because you're dumb? Because you're gullible? Because you're careless? Some of us are all of these. But most of us are simply too busy or too tired or too harrassed to take a computer, a slide rule, and an M.I.T. graduate to market and figure out what we're buying. And the makers of the goods we buy know this. In fact they know far more about us than we know about them. They have spent millions of dollars studying us—the consumer. They know what colors and what sizes and what shapes and what words we go for. Compared to them the Big Brother in George Orwell's "1984," who knows all and sees all, is a piker. The Big Brothers in our society today are not government dictators: they are the sellers and their brainwashing handmaidens, the behavioral scientists. Together, and under the banner of free choice and open competition, they have made us believe that we are getting what we pay for. Their purpose is that innocent goal of free enterprise—to make an extra buck. But when their profit becomes our loss, how innocent is that goal? And what is our loss?

Not much, you may say. An ounce here, a cent there, and what real difference does it make? Most of us have learned to accept the added charges of packaging and advertising and distribution along with the product. But must we pay for deception too?

Just take one figure—baby foods again. Remember the brand where you paid the same price as you used to but got a quarter ounce less food? Well, if your baby ate four jars of this applesauce or carrot puree a day, he would eat twenty-four pounds less food per year—without your knowing it. Do you care? Does it matter?

Maybe it doesn't. We are a spoiled and lazy and wasteful people; our pay checks were never higher and so what—that's the way business is done. A little less applesauce, a few less crackers, a few more pennies here and there: who cares?

But it isn't a question of applesauce. It's a question of morality. Little deceptions of single consumers can add up to a mighty deception of a whole people. You may only lose a penny here and there, but the loss in dollars sustained daily by American consumers who pay for more than they get is estimated to be greater than the staggering amount we forfeit to crime and corruption. But it's not sensational. It doesn't hit the headlines. And who is going to bring it to your attention? The press which depends on advertising? Television which owes its existence to products? The makers of the products? As Eliza Doolittle said in *Pygmalion*, "Not Bloody Likely!"

Only those whose prime concern is people and not profit can tell us the score: organizations like the Consumers Union and those agencies of government who regulate the pure and basic world of weights and measures and law and justice, so that the exchange of goods is a transaction of trust.

But we, the public, have got to want to know the score. If we don't care, nobody else will care. Dishonest practices, because they succeed, will drive out honest practices, because they don't. In the end, our condition depends entirely on us. And I think at last we may be beginning to realize it.

The murmur of rebellion against these widespread deceptions and confusions in packaging is swelling daily. People *are* bringing their slide rules to market, they *are* taking a good look at what the package says and what it holds, they *are* beginning to write protests to the manufacturers who manipulate them. But still not enough.

We hear day in and day out of the revolutions that are sweeping the world. I think we are ripe for one here. And when you hear the testimony that follows in this chamber, I believe you will think we are ripe for one too—a revolution of the American consumer against the manipulation of his mind and money by practices of packaging and labeling that empty his purse and his market basket while he is looking the other way.

So far the manufacturers guilty of these deceptions are not the majority; yet among them are some of the most respected brand names in the business. They will, of course, deny deliberate deception and produce any number of reasons which they consider both valid and legal for packaging and labeling as they do. But the evidence stands and the confusion mounts.

Ladies and gentlemen—Consumers—we *are* being kidded. In the days of McCarthy, Elmer Davis said of those who tried to confuse our thinking, "Don't let them scare you." Today I would like to say of those who try to confuse our buying and our values, "Don't let them kid you."

And I kid you not.

PASSING THE BUCK IN CONGRESS

NOTE: In January of 1964, the Women's National Press Club gave one of its annual dinners welcoming the return of members of Congress to the capital. This was one of four speeches addressed to an audience composed of Senators, Representatives, and other top-ranking government officials.

SINCE THIS OCCASION was presumably intended to look hopefully to a New Year, imagine my dismay at being given a topic called "The Moral and Ethical Challenge of '64." With sinking heart, I saw myself dressed in an iron corset, long bloomers, and a boned high neck brandishing an umbrella in your faces as I invoked fire and brimstone on your sinning heads.

The trouble is, I guess I had it coming to me. I have recently committed two pieces of fire and brimstone for a thin little intellectual magazine called McCall's. The last one, on Corruption,

Supermarket

was tastefully sandwiched between Diaper Service and Senator Goldwater; the next one, on Violence, will doubtless share billing with Glazed Ham and Frigidity. But strange bedfellows notwithstanding (do bedfellows stand?), I meant what I said. And what I said was that we are both a corrupt and violent society, that it's been creeping up on us for a long time now, and that unless we do something about it, we've got something in our midst much more to be feared than communism—and that thing is anarchy.

Now I can't in all honesty say that we'll *have* anarchy in '64, but I can't in all honesty say that we'll be less corrupt and violent next year than last year. I wish I could. I wish I could feel that a nation sobered by great tragedy would have undergone a major purification instead of a temporary revulsion from evil.

But memory is short, the country is full of nuts—some of them in politics—and the call of the fast buck is still loud in the land. For the pursuit of this fast buck, anything goes. And if anyone wants to get a real loud laugh in this society of ours, all he has to say is "honesty is the best policy." Saddest of all—some of us are old enough to have once believed it.

Speaking of which, I got a letter from a stranger the other day who'd heard me sound off on ethics on some radio program. I'd like to pass on a few of the things he said:

"Once a person starts earning a living," he wrote, "the manner in which he handles his business problems are of *prior* importance. Please note," he said, "that I said Prior—not necessarily more important. I am seventy-one and was brought up on the same 'honesty is the best policy' teaching that you were. You said in substance that success may take longer for the ethical person, financially, but at least he can live with himself with a clear conscience. I wish it were as simple as that."

"Take the price-fixing scandal which sent a few corporation executives to jail," said the letter. "Now supposing some of these men were faced with the prospect of either getting fired for not getting enough business or entering into rigged bidding. The point is, has a man the right to practice a strict code of ethics at the expense of his family obligations?"

43

But Will It Sell?

And he winds up by saying "Expediency is the price of survival."

Maybe he's right. But survival on what terms? What kind of woman, what kind of children would rather have a crook for a husband and father than do without the second car or the mink coat? Are we really producing a race that says "it doesn't matter how you get it so long as we have it?" Is this the great and glorious future of our democracy—that the end is money, and the means don't matter?

Has a man the right to practice a strict code of ethics at the expense of his family obligations? What a strange way to put it —has a man the *right*? I would think he had the *obligation* to himself and his family to be an honorable man, and if this meant that his son had to earn his way through college and his wife couldn't afford new slipcovers—so what? Wouldn't this living example of honor and ethics be worth more to his family and his community than a few extra thousand a year in income? Or have we sunk so low that the only principle that counts ends with an *-al?*

Of course, when I say We, I'm not speaking of our honored guests tonight. Everyone knows that the representatives of the people are not truly representative. That they are immune to the temptations that make the rest of us so corrupt. No member of Congress, in Senate or House, has ever put private favors above public interest or voted for a bill not because he thought it right but because it would help re-elect him. None of you have ever succumbed to the pressures of private interests or used influence for a man who could be useful to you, or traveled anywhere on public expense, or added a member of the family to your payroll. None of you own broadcasting stations or newspapers that might assist your public career—what is that phrase?—conflict of interest? And certainly none of you have ever kept a bill from reaching the floor because you didn't want it put to a vote, or have ever had fun and games at the taxpayer's expense: private enterprise pays for your private pleasures.

So I don't really know what I'm doing talking about the Moral and Ethical Challenge of the New Year to the honorable men of Congress. The people of the United States expect you to be just as chaste, as honest, as altruistic, as courageous, as logical, as open-minded, and as close-mouthed in 1964 as you were in 1963.

If you're not, don't blame us for sinking into the state of anarchy I've been warning about. Because if we catch you putting your constituents' votes above your country's interests, it's only natural that we will go on putting our private incomes above the public good. We look to you, gentlemen, to give us some proof that morality and ethics are more essential to survival than expediency.

2: *For Husbands and Lovers*

PREFACE

THERE IS A QUAINT ASSUMPTION in this country that what concerns women is of interest only to women. The women's pages of newspapers and magazines amply confirm this, the reason being that virile men are not and should not be interested in food, clothes, decoration, furnishings, or female personalities. In fact, the word "women" (as opposed to "girls") in a title or headline is supposed to make the reading male flip over the page in boredom or aversion and in search of subjects worthier of his attention. It is hard enough to live with them (he might be saying) without reading about them.

What is more, it has been considered winsome in a man to confess that he doesn't understand women. (This is in "The ladies—God bless 'em!" tradition.) We suggest he try. For he would find us far more like himself—with many of the same needs, drives, and dreams—than he has long chosen to believe.

The revolution of the sexes, well under way but still strongly resisted, is simply this: that the biological difference is no longer the dominant factor in the composition of personality, and will, with the help of science, steadily diminish as a limitation of capacity. A woman then will be a single human being before she is a wife or a mother, just as a man has always been a separate entity besides being a husband or father.

What concerns us here is this equality of identity: quite another matter than those familiar bugbears, Rivalry and Competition, by which the emancipation of women is supposed to have poisoned the natural relationship of the sexes.

Dear Men: we love you; we like to make you happy; we usually want to bear your children. But if the price of living with you is supporting your illusions about us, it is becoming too high for some of us. The death of marriage is the mutual deception practiced for single advantage. Whether it is the man who pretends he is strong or the woman who pretends she is weak, both in the end betray themselves and each other. The highest compliment we can pay you as men is to want you to be as you really are. We ask the same of you.

We are neither accessories, instruments, nor objects, although in the wide range from housekeeper to whore we have for a very long time been used as such. The analogy between women and Negroes is not so farfetched as it might seem: our physical characteristics have come between us and our full development as human beings. If Negroes were happy on benevolent plantations, as white men said they were, it could have been because they had no way of knowing what, freed, they were capable of. And if women are happy (as most of them have long been assumed to be) in kitchen and playroom, it may well be because they do not yet know the larger dimensions within and outside of themselves. The cage is not the plantation fence or the suburban wall, but the image drawn of some by the minds of others. The image is the child of social convenience: of the whites in the case of Negroes, of men in the case of women. When the image is shattered, society suffers the dislocation natural to revolution and growth. The status quo is dearest to those who benefit by it.

But resistance to change is a losing battle, and in the follow-ing piece I try to explain why. It was originally a speech de-livered at the University of California College of Medicine in San Francisco, and it addressed itself not to all women but to a relatively small proportion of us. Yet it struck an answering chord in so many that it has, one hopes, a wider application and implication. It should in any case give men some explanation of why a growing number of us are as we are—and how to deal with it!

When you have recovered from it, you can be comforted by two pieces, in flirtation and love, which admit freely that biological differences are—if not dominant—fun.

As for the last piece, on the elevation of the young to a posi-tion in society far beyond their deserts, you men might well preserve it as a father's weapon against a child's usurpation. Adults, arise!

THE SINGULAR WOMAN

MANY TIMES during this examina-tion of a certain kind of woman and the world she lives in, I have asked myself: who cares? It is not merely that creative women—those who can produce intellectually and artistically as well as biologically—are a minority, constituting a very small portion of the female population of this country. It is, I am reluctantly convinced, that they are neither particularly wanted nor particularly valued. Oh, you and I have read scores of articles these last years about the great wasted reservoir of female intelligence, about the nation's need not only for educated women but for thinking women trained and ready to apply their knowledge and skills in professions that presumably cry for them. But if the call is there, I have not heard it. And if the need is there, society—and that includes women—either ignores it or rejects it.

This rejection has been confirmed by fact as well as inferred by personal experience. Not long ago *The New York Times* published an article on the job status of women in which Martin Tolchin wrote: "The educated women of America have lost ground in their attempt to place their talent at the disposal of a nation that professes to be hungry for brainpower." And later on he says, "The decline of the professional women has been attributed to a combination of factors that include earlier marriages, misuse of education, job discrimination, and what Mary I. Bunting, President of Radcliffe College, calls 'hidden persuaders . . . the cultural forces that tell a woman it is unladylike to use her mind.'" I would add that all these factors stem from one major cause: fear. Fear in both men and women of the next step in the continuing revolution they prefer to ignore—steps which I rashly intend to define.

For what I write from now on will be subjective: the result of my own experience and observation, for I *am* a woman and I *think* I am creative. And although dozens of books and hundreds of papers and articles have been written by many wise and wiser people on this subject, and although some of what they have said will be echoed by me, I choose to ignore them now. What is more, I am sick, as a woman, of being talked about and written about, especially by men who can not feel what we feel, or by women who are not what we are. And the only reason that I am adding more words to this subject is that I feel it high time to think radically and in new terms, to clear away what I consider to be a thicket of misconceptions and timidities, and to open a window in the suffocating room of our present social

For Husbands and Lovers

patterning. Some of my ideas, therefore, are bound to be unpalatable, if not repellent, to the majority of our citizens who believe that prosperity and procreation—in wedlock, of course—are the only valid goals of man and woman. I happen to think that there are other goals as valid, and as valuable, both for man and woman.

How did I get that way? Well, I saw it around me when I was a small child. My mother and father were both concert musicians and both teachers, my mother of the piano, my father of the violin. There was nothing strange whatever to me in the fact that my mother, a woman, spent much of each day practicing or giving lessons, that she often went off on tour with my father, and that she couldn't boil an egg. She didn't have to. In the early part of the twentieth century even people of very modest means had cooks and nurses, and it was taken equally for granted by my brother and myself that if our mother was away, the cook, the nurse, or the great-aunt who lived with us, would take care of us. There was no sense of rejection, no shocks at being "motherless" for a period of weeks. Life went on fully; we studied, ate, and slept, and when our parents did come back we were delighted to see them.

It was also quite natural to me that, besides being an artist of real distinction, my mother created an extremely attractive home, took care of all my impractical father's personal needs, entertained scores of fellow musicians, and was, for all her attainments, intensely feminine and maternal.

Now you can say two things that I, as a child, did not then realize. One was that my mother was an exceptional woman. The other was that servants and relatives made it possible for her to maintain a professional life and a domestic life without harm to either. Both were true. I can add one more thing: that the temper of the time was different. The mass media had not enthroned the housewife as God's noblest creature and best consumer, reams of nonsense were not being written about woman's proper rôle, and women themselves did not regard professional or career women with that mixture of envy, disapproval, and superiority which seems to color contemporary social attitudes. Women like my mother were then, as they are now, a minority, but an accepted and admired one.

It was therefore quite natural that I should grow up believing that all was possible for a girl or woman. Certainly, both my father and brother made it seem so. Both spoke to me as equals of many things that girls are not supposed to be interested in. My brother passed on to me the first principles of physics, the relativity of time, and how to throw a curve with a baseball. My father discussed with me, from the age of ten years onward, such things as the nature of melancholy, how to get a vibrato on a violin, and how sickness could be caused by states of mind. I lived, therefore, for over seventeen years in the world of imagination and discovery, going steady not with the boy next door but the men out of range. I was passionately in love with Julius Caesar, Hamlet, Henry V of England, and John Barrymore of Hollywood. I did not start transferring my affections to more attainable men until I was nineteen, at which point I threw away the books along with self-restraint.

But at no time, then or since, did I throw away a sense of fierce independence as a human being and the desire to attain distinction in terms of mind and spirit and expression. Since I wanted to undergo the full range of human experience, the thought that my sex should confine me exclusively to wifehood, motherhood, and domesticity was untenable. I did not even, at that early age, want children. I wanted that splendid but impossible thing called freedom. I still do, but I know where it is—within—and how hard it has to be fought for.

Now I have dwelt on this background not because it was right for a woman or natural for a woman, but because it was right and natural for the kind of human being I happen to be. I suspect it to be considerably more common than is generally recognized. It took me a good many years to figure out what that is and why it is. It is something which others might define in the precise terms of their professional knowledge but which I can only describe very simply as this: that each human being, male or female, is composed of both male and female components and that the proportion of one to the other varies widely in each person. While the public generally assumes that all normal women are, or should be, a hundred per cent female, the truth is that a woman can be seventy or even sixty per cent female to thirty or forty per cent male and still function biologically as a woman, with all the physical attributes which this entails.

Yet together with these functions and attributes, the woman with a higher quotient of masculine qualities must function also on other levels, whether it is in the world of ideas or performance, or in the expression of sexual drives not necessarily linked to procreation. Such women can love men yet not submerge themselves in men, can love children but not dedicate themselves to them, can enjoy domesticity but not devote themselves to it, can be feminine but not make a fetish of it. In so being, they may miss the intense pleasures of submission, the unity of character and the security of rôle which the "normal" women enjoy, but they can also gain that breadth of experience, intellectual and emotional, that free and single identity which their majority of sisters are often denied.

But the women who feel compelled towards creative expression, whether in the arts or sciences, in exploration and adventure, in the battles of politics and government, must learn to accept the losses which accompany these gains. And here we come to the basic root of the problem confronting men and women today: acceptance not of what society *thinks* we should be but what we really are. Everything I have said about creative women applies equally to noncompetitive men: the dreamers rather than the doers, the non-go-getters, the sensitive and gentle men who possess a higher-than-average proportion of female components without being in any sense effeminate. Equipped neither as fighters nor, primarily, as breadwinners, lacking the desire to impose their will on others or to dominate the women they love, they are in their own way as valuable to society as their "normal" aggressive brothers.

The trouble is, I think, that this complexity of rôles within men and women—the result of a slow, long, but dramatic revolution in the sexes—has not been realized by the public as a whole. Or if it has been subconsciously recognized, it has been consciously rejected. Why? Because it challenges the whole structure of marriage, the family, society as we now know it. It challenges a good many time-worn assumptions that have been not only comfortable for men but convenient for the majority of women, too.

For equality is not at issue here. Equal franchise, equal pay, the end of legal and civil discriminations against women have been, though fought for, inevitable. What is at issue is the recognition of minorities, among which creative women and nonaggressive men are the largest—far larger, I repeat than we think. That this recognition must extend to, and include, the homosexuals at either end of the spectrum, goes without saying. Whether these manifestations of human complexity or, if you will, deviation, are desirable is not the question either. They exist, they are here, they will not go away, they may even increase. The point is to make them productive instead of destructive, to recognize what values they have, to incorporate them openly and without prejudice into our society. For it is the refusal to accept and even value their difference from the norm that causes unhappiness and ultimately harm: the problems which I am here confining to the creative woman.

What exactly are these problems? The earliest, I would think, are her parents. From infancy they give her no choice to be anything but what they think a girl should be. They smother her in pink when she might prefer blue, they give her dolls when she might prefer trains, they present her with books about girls when she might rather read about boys, and they send her to a psychiatrist if she, at sixteen, likes books better than boys. Now, in fact, they initiate the mating process when she is twelve in the firm conviction that the only possible future for her is early marriage, lots of children, and a suburban home. If their girl shows a desire to paint or model or write verse, the more intelligent parents, of course, encourage her. A talent is fine so long as it is kept within bounds—meaning youthful expression before the real business of being a woman takes over. It is far more disturbing if the female over eighteen still wants to be a doctor, or a biologist, or a lawyer, although parents can comfort themselves with the hope that when she meets budding doctors, biologists, and lawyers in the course of her studies, she will choose the husband rather than the profession.

But even if her parents, as were mine, are proud of her intellectual curiosity, her talent, her independence of spirit, and encourage them, she can never escape the relentless, steady nudging of society: the assumption that she is in some way unfeminine, that she is jeopardizing her future happiness as a woman, that what she is doing is merely a substitute for her true, and only valid, functions. Everything she sees about her, moreover, seems to confirm this assumption. From childhood through adolescence the women all around her—her mother, her neighbor, her best friend's mother—are home-bound and house-oriented to a degree not even experienced by *their* own mothers, and certainly not dreamed of by those valiant pioneers of sixty years ago whose militant efforts to widen women's horizons and take them *out* of the kitchen earned them ridicule along with rights. They must be turning in their graves to see most of their female descendants not only being full-time servants to their many children and to their houses, but serene in their sense of superiority over their career-bound sisters.

The housewife image, moreover, is exalted daily by all the mass media which find in the young, large, solvent family an inexhaustible market. In television soap operas the apron is the mark of a good woman, the career the sign of a frustrated one, the single existence the proof of a desperate one. In the fiction in the mass women's magazines the heroine is never brilliant, original, creative, or ambitious. In all the ads in all the media, woman steps out of her four-walled rôle only long enough to drive the car to school, to the hairdresser, or to market.

Irresistibly, the American girl is formed into this image from childhood, and by the time she is going steady at twelve, her future is so clearly indicated that only exceptional will and courage can change it. For the risk of changing it is loss of popularity which in turn is loss of femininity which in turn has been drummed into her as acquired characteristics of dressing, make-up, attitude, and talk that mark her as desirable. Clearly listed as undesirable in this lexicon of attraction are independence of mind, intellectual ambition, and attachment to work.

So our girl in this free country has, in truth, little choice. Security is the goal, and as soon as possible. Marry the boy right away, get the house right away, have the brood right away. No time for search of self, no time for experiments in love and life, no time for interior growth, no time for the great world outside.

Now what is wrong with that, you say? The majority of women since time began have found their greatest fulfillment in the home as wife and mother. If they hadn't, the race would have perished. Why grudge them their happiness just because it isn't yours?

I do not grudge them their happiness. I merely question whether a number of them are indeed happy: whether given a real choice by a more fluid society they might not be better doctors than mothers, better mathematicians than home-makers, better courtesans than wives. I could question equally whether a number of the young men trapped into domesticity and corporations at twenty would not be happier explorers than fathers, poets than husbands, and rakes than lawnmowers.

Ah, says society, but what about the continuance of the race, what about the structure of the family, what about the sanctity of marriage? Again, I find myself—in the light of the present —questioning whether the profound changes working on all three are either understood or accepted as reality demands that they should be.

Has not, for instance, unlimited procreation become a danger as great, or greater, than the bomb? Is not the large family now an indulgence rather than a duty—a luxury for which the children themselves will pay with intolerable congestion, inadequate schooling, and the deprivation of those amenities and pleasures which make for civilized living? Is a proliferation of babies more important to the race now than the development of intelligence? And if all these questions suggest that man and woman may have reached a stage where love has other goals besides procreation, should they not be recognized as valid and therefore acceptable?

Whether they are or not, they exist. Nature has ways of adjusting herself to the realities. The world can sustain many different kinds of love, whether it is between man and man, a relationship that has often been culturally productive; between woman and woman; between man and mistress. All, in a sense, are in revolt against a society so overwhelmingly swaddled in domestic units that it can not see beyond the next mortgage or the next car to the next holocaust. All are in revolt against concepts of the correct and normal rôles for men and women which bear no relation to the sexual duality inherent in a great many people.

Of these the creative woman is, as I've said, a prime example. And her problems are not as inherent in her nature as in her relationship to a society which accepts her only on certain conditions. It is her attempt to gain this acceptance by fulfilling these conditions that makes for trouble.

Let's look at some of them. Nobody objects to a woman being a good writer or sculptor or geneticist if at the same time she manages to be a good wife, a good mother, good-looking, good-tempered, well-dressed, well-groomed, and unaggressive. These are the entrance charges for the approval of other men and women. They are, I maintain, exorbitant to the point of impossibility. Nobody expected George Eliot to be a beauty. Nobody worried about Jeanne d'Arc's haircut. Emily Dickinson was not scorned for being childless. Nobody urged Marie Curie to dye her hair.

I was interested to see photographs of Dr. Kelsey, who did so much to keep the drug thalidomide out of the country. It was clear that a woman of that degree of dedication to her work didn't have the time to have her hair colored or spend hours shopping. Why should she be expected to? Yet we think we are,

But Will It Sell?

because of one thing only: the fear that men will reject us. Thanks largely to the brilliant manipulation of mass media, women are obsessed with an ideal of femininity as the guarantee of happiness. Be thin, be smart, be gay, be sexy, be soft-spoken. Get new slipcovers, learn new recipes, have bright children, further your man's career, help the community, drive the car, smile. And if you can write a best seller or a Broadway hit, too, that's great.

There are some women who manage to do just that, and they fill me with awe and envy. But most of us who produce in the realm of thought and ideas can not do and be all these things and should not try. Evidence abounds that even the supposedly contented suburban housewife with four children and no aspirations beyond her home is a victim of this multiplicity of rôles. In the process of trying to be a mother, wife, lover, chef, servant, and hostess, she apparently consumes alarming quantities of tranquillizers and alcohol—surely not an index of fulfillment. Yet those of us who aspire creatively struggle as she does to prove to the world that we too are feminine and, therefore, desirable.

This, I maintain, is a sort of craven appeasement that does no honor to a free intelligence. For, the fact is, we can not have our cake and eat it too. We can not enjoy our mobility, our resources, our liberties, our triumphs, our intense and heady involvements without paying for them. And these are some of the prices: the first is popularity. At school, the brilliant, intense girl student with dreams in her head isn't going to get the boys unless her attractions are strong enough to deceive them. In this case she will probably get the wrong boys, for the right ones won't be ready for her. Beauty is possibly the greatest hazard of a creative woman— to herself as well as to its victims. Male adoration is a powerful deterrent to female sense, and it is extremely difficult to tear one's self from loving arms and say, "Sorry, darling, I've got to work." It is so much easier and pleasanter to drown in current delights than gird for future dreams. Also, beauty demands a degree of maintenance, and it is the strong woman who turns her back on the hairdresser to gain two extra hours of work. Certainly, creative labor has been a compensation in many women of talent for the attractions they lack, and there is no doubt that homeliness permits a dedication and continuity which beauty fragments. In this case, the advance of middle age can be a boon: as the lines increase, the distractions dwindle, and seduction can be more easily confined to the typewriter or microscope.

After school or college, the creative young woman seriously concerned with work will have to realize that marriage with the wrong man can be worse than no marriage. While all her sisters are marching down the aisle at nineteen and twenty for the sake of being married, she must have the nerve to resist the stampede and give herself time to learn, to experience, to grow in the direction of her free dreams. Above all, she must not be afraid of singleness or even loneliness, for I know of no woman, let alone man, who has any stature or worth without knowledge of either. It is the insecure and the immature who can not bear the thought of their own singularity, who must hold on to another hand from puberty onward, who surround themselves with human buffers against the world.

Since vitality and curiosity are essential equipments of a creative woman, she must be willing to pay the price of trial and error—loving men who may not love her, being loved by men she can not love. If she is worried about what others think of her, by what standards of morality she is judged, she will not stand the gaff of independence long.

If she marries, soon or late, she will be wise to find the man with sufficient female sensitivity to match her masculine liberty; for the kind of man who has to prove his masculinity through domination is not for her. She will therefore be inordinately lucky if she finds one of the relatively few men whose security lies in the full and equal partnership of a love which may—or may not—produce children.

If she has children, this creative woman of ours, she must pay for this indulgence with a long burden of guilt, for her life will be split three ways between her children, her husband, and her work. What she gives to one, she must take from the other, and there will be no time when one or the other is not harmed. No woman with any heart can compose a paragraph when her child is in trouble or her husband ill: forever they take precedence over the companions of her mind. In this, as in many other things, the creative woman has a much tougher time than the creative man. For one thing, she has no wife, as he has, to protect her from intrusion, to maintain the machinery of living, to care for the children, to answer the doorbell. For another, no one believes her time to be sacred. A man at his desk in a room with a closed door is a man at work. A woman at a desk in any room is available.

Now, most of us learn to accept this if we want both worlds of wife and work. The only alternative is to relinquish marriage in favor of men. I am quite serious about this interesting possibility: the recognition and acceptance of a special category of woman not unlike the hetaerae of Periclean Athens: women who concentrate on the arts of mind and body for the delectation of brilliant men—and themselves. Brought up to date, I see this as a chance for the inspired female to work alone all day and have companionship at night with a variety of men, similar only in that their need for stimulation is intellectual as well as physical. This would relieve them at intervals from the boredom of domesticity and rescue them gracefully from more sordid outlets! It would not be popular with wives, although it would relieve *them* in turn of their responsibility to be glamorous and amorous as well as motherly and wifely. But perhaps I am a bit ahead of myself—and the times!

Where were we? Ah, yes, the penalties of being a creative female. One of them concerns nomenclature. The gentlemen of the press carefully refrain from identifying a man as a Negro or a woman as a Negress, but rarely hesitate to call a woman a poetess or a sculptress, antique phrases that suggest Victorian females painting on china. Even worse, a highly sophisticated magazine like *The New Yorker* delights in referring to "lady poets" or "lady playwrights," titles of spurious and ponderous gallantry which reveal nothing less than contempt. Have you ever read of a gentleman writer?—or even a man writer? There is also a tendency in male reviewers to describe any novel written by a woman and dealing with the sensibilities of women as "a woman's book." This assumption that women are interesting only to women is as silly as the assumption that men are interesting only to men. Since neither of these assumptions exist in European literary attitudes, they appear to be largely of Anglo-Saxon origin, reflecting, I suggest, an astounding lack of communication between our men and women except on sexual levels. Why should not a man be as intensely interested in a woman's clothes, thoughts, desires, dreams as she should be in a man's? Where does the embarrassment come in?

We now come to certain social problems which may seem equally trivial but which, over a period of time, erode the tissues of the professional female. Let us say that a woman has been a successful writer for over twenty years under the name of Jane Smith. Ten years ago she married a man called John Cooper. She is henceforth introduced at social gatherings as Mrs. Cooper. A lot of people know about Jane Smith. Nobody knows about Mrs. Cooper. Certainly not the other professionals at the party who know Jane Smith but don't know she's Mrs. Cooper. Result: no contact, desultory conversation with strangers, dull time. Why? Because the hostess has no imagination, because convention dies hard, because it takes that tiny added trouble to say, "Mr. and Mrs. Cooper—Jane Smith." As a matter of fact, along with the revival of the hetaerae we might adopt the Spanish idea of hyphenating the husband's and wife's name. I have always found the obliteration of the wife's name an outmoded custom related to chattels, property, and such. Since the mark of the individual is identity, why submerge it? Has any man, distinguished in his field as John Smith, imagined the sensation of being introduced to colleagues or strangers by his wife's name? Another social custom I find equally antique: the segregation of women from men after dinner. I share wholeheartedly Senator Maurine Neuberger's frustration at being separated from the best male minds for the balance of an evening.

But Will It Sell?

But here, of course, we get at the root of the matter. It is widely assumed, by both men and women, that men feel more comfortable without the presence of women. This is certainly true of the upper-class British and of the more socially conventional Americans. Why? Because they want to tell dirty jokes? That has long since ceased to be a male prerogative. Because women are not intellectually up to their talk? Hardly, because many women now are. Yet only intelligent men seek the company of intelligent women. The majority avoid what they think of as competition. They don't want some female deeply acquainted with foreign affairs to question their views on Berlin. They don't want any woman to tell them anything. What is asserted by a man is an opinion; what is asserted by a woman is opinionated. A woman with ideas and the ability to express them is something of a social embarrassment, like an unhousebroken pet. People like us, therefore, must learn to keep a respectful silence in the presence of men who may have a higher but also a lower intelligence, or speak our minds at the risk of the glassy male eye. So here we are again, supposedly intelligent and gifted women, scared of losing our femininity by the simple measure of saying what we think—and know. How much safer to play the rôle assigned us by the experts, to be still, to know our place, to charm—even to lie?

But since the urge to create is a search for truth, the lie does not work. We are hoist by our own honesty, by our singularity, by our identity. And yet without them none of us would be any good in the work we choose to do. That is our problem.

But why should it concern society, of which we are such a minority? Because I believe this minority to be in the vanguard of the revolution which the majority are now resisting. In fact, the American counterrevolution is a phenomenon which no one has yet explained to my satisfaction. While most other civilized countries, from Britain to Scandinavia to the Soviet Union, are incorporating more and more women of high intellectual attainments in their major professions and positions, the United States is plunged into an orgy of domesticity and childbearing. While day nurseries to take care of the children of professional women are standard community services in these countries, they are still viewed here as a Communist plot against the family and motherhood. While it is a matter of course to find brilliant women statesmen, doctors, university professors, and scientists elsewhere, they are as rare as trumpeter swans over here. The exceptionally gifted and articulate woman in the United States usually finds herself the only woman in symposia and conferences, on panels and discussion groups. This could be called token integration— a delaying device which is supposed to answer certain needs and objections without actually facing the root of the problem. It is no particular satisfaction to the intelligent and articulate woman to stick out like a sore thumb, or, if you will, like a jewelled forefinger.

It is time that society was trained to think differently about its men and women if the whole question of female identity as independent human beings is to be given the importance it deserves.

The first change must come about in women themselves. Those with a strong talent and a consistent desire for creative expression must stop trying to discourage and suppress their aspirations by attempting to conform to society's image of a woman or to "please" a man. If a man does not love a woman *because* of this independence, he is not for her.

As for men, they will have to wake up to the fact that for many women, the need for a separate identity is as important to them as their identity as wife and mother. They should also learn that creativity and femininity are not only compatible but often inseparable, that a body with a brain can be more responsive than a body without, and that imagination is the sister of love. Admittedly, the recognition of these truths by men is not made any easier in a society where intellectuality is suspect from adolescence, and where adolescent attitudes are cherished into middle age.

In planning a family, both men and women must come to realize that on this explosively overcrowded planet, the quality of their children is of far greater value to society than their quantity. Self-restraint may be alien to the human temperament, but humanity without restraint will dig its own grave.

Ironically, the large family is now not only considered a status symbol but has made the single or childless woman an object of derogation and pity—attitudes immensely destructive to her self-respect and happiness.

Once the large family is considered an indulgence rather than a contribution, the productive values of the single woman can be recognized, and she, free from the sense of guilt and inadequacy that now haunts her, can divert her full energies to the many crying needs of society. That the word "single woman" or "spinster" should imply inferior worth or usefulness is only one of the damaging by-products of our present consumer-based, security-mad, domestic pattern.

Finally, the people who deal in mass media must recognize that out of millions of women who are entirely happy and fulfilled in their classic rôles as wife and mother, there are thousands who are not; and that they may represent productive values of equal use to society and the nation.

In the meantime, and pending these changes towards an adult, rather than an adolescent, society, the lonely few of us will just have to go on being ourselves: living our special kind of life to the fullest, accepting responsibility for what we lack as well as for what we give, and taking the sniping from those who deplore us as well as the praise of those who admire us. Above all, we are not to be either feared or pitied. We made our beds, and although they are sometimes hard, they are good for the spine—and the spirit. Most women would not want to trade places with us, but some women who question their own aspirations may now be encouraged to pursue them. For it takes courage to know what you are—and to be what you are: yourself.

A PLEA FOR FLIRTATION

IN AN AGE where the lowered eye-
lid is merely a sign of fatigue, the delicate game of love is pining
away. This observation may, of course, be traced to the age of
the writer and countered by an army of women under forty who
find, in this country of youth, no such decline in the practice
of flirtation.

But I doubt it. While so much of our life is confined to halfway
measures (the middle-of-the-road is the security zone), love
is the exception. A man and a woman are either in love or just
friends. And this, I think, is a very great pity. For I remember
from earlier years, as I know from present experience abroad,
a highly stimulating area between these extremes in which the
presence of sex in conversation can be a pleasure in itself, making a man feel more of a man and a woman more of a woman
without requiring either mating or marriage. It can, in fact, be
enjoyed by those happily married to others, by those maintaining,
for whatever reason, a single state, and by those with dishonor-
able intentions. Flirtation is merely an expression of considered
desire coupled with an admission of its impracticability. "I think
you are very attractive," say the eyes of man to the eyes of
woman, "and it would be nice if we could. But you know and I
know we can't."

"If we were on a desert island together," say the eyes of
woman to the eyes of man, "we could have a very pleasant time."
In a good flirtation these semaphores are never translated into
words. In fact, they may be waved back and forth during a conversation on theatre, pink-foot geese, or skindiving, though talk

67

of the stock market might prove too competitive. (Money is not an aphrodisiac: the desire it may kindle in the female eye is more for the cash than the carrier.)

But if it is indeed true that these passages of arms and eyes are increasingly rare in our social life today, what are the reasons? We can eliminate those groups in which flirtation never flourished, and one of them is what we are now allowed to call "the lower economic bracket." They want what they want when they want it, and that's about it. And if we are to believe the dialogue of Paddy Chayefsky and other tape-recorder writers, words are out of the picture. Or rather, they come singly and painfully between man and woman as they shuffle toward a disordered bed. Not for them the time or the taste for sweet nothings; or the vocabulary.

And what of the middle bracket of our people, the happy suburbans? Well, it's hard to flirt with the kiddies underfoot, and if one is to believe what one reads about life in Oakwood, adults are never alone until after their third Martini, when lunges towards the neighbor's wife come under the heading of euphoria rather than flirtation. Alcohol, no matter where, precipitates the behavior which a controlled flirtation would evade. You can't be tight and tentative.

And what of the leisured people, the upper bracket, the intellectuals? Well, I would cancel out the contemporary intellectuals in our society: a great many seem to think that a free spirit and social graces are incompatible, and they find the frivolity of a compliment beneath them. I think also that Freud and flirtation are poor companions, for a search for meanings can spoil a lot of fun.

So now we come to the last rampart, the arbiters, the traveled, the sophisticated. We are not talking here of the young in search of marriage: their flirtations have deadly purpose. We are talking of those ostensibly stabilized, if not trapped.

Well, I have been to a legion of dinners with people like these, and I find the pattern between men and women something like this: if the man you sit next to is an old friend, familiarity precludes flirtation; you talk of friends or weekend traffic. You can't be both cosy and curious, and curiosity is a major ingredient in flirtation. If the man you sit next to is an old beau who still finds you attractive, he will usually be too fond of your husband and too afraid of his wife to say so. Affection for the mates of others is the Great Neutralizer.

If the man you sit next to is a stranger—presumably the ideal beginning—you have three problems as a woman. If you try to entertain him, he is inclined to think you are either garrulous or aggressive. If you wait for him to entertain you, the woman on his other side will grab him. And if you betray any interest in him as a man, panic will seize him (watch out for this woman). Your neighbor may be masterful on the golf course, but the fairways of flirtation are for him a terrain of hazards for which he is not equipped. More profoundly, what generic love of women and interest in women he may once have had has been long since overlaid by paper work: he has forgotten how to talk to women unless they are secretaries.

Unlike Europeans, then, our American man is more relieved than dismayed when the host bears him off to the company of men after dinner, and the women are segregated, spending together what seems to be the balance of the night. Whatever mood was established during cocktails and dinner is never recaptured after the sexes, at long last, are rejoined. The male eyes are on the wrist watch, the female eyes on their husbands, and the only semaphores waved spell "Let's go home."

Cocktail parties—particularly large ones—are better for flirting, although hostesses have a compulsive genius for discouraging its development. No sooner have you established some contact with your partner's eye and mind, than she pulls you away to meet a couple who are welded to each other by timidity as well as marriage. There is nothing more annoying, in fact, to the average hostess, than an unmated couple enjoying each other's company.

But Will It Sell?

Now, travel used to be a magnificent field for flirtation and, in other parts of the world, still is. It is possible, if not inevitable, to play this game of attraction on a train or plane crossing the boundaries of Europe and carrying men of curiosity and courage; but something strange has happened to that former cradle of flirtation: the ocean liner.

Pick-ups, yes. You have only to stand at the rail of a ship alone for a while to have some man inch up alongside and break the silence. But always the wrong man with the wrong voice. Why? Because the attractive man, the desirable man, the right man, is in mortal terror of speaking to, or being spoken to by, the wrong woman. So, plunged in a book in remote deck chair behind a stanchion, or holed in his cabin till the last day, he keeps himself inviolate. Now this, of course, is not always the case. He may quite possibly engage in flirtation with a woman who is the wrong one merely because she is not yourself. (You call her The Obvious Type: Lays it on with a Trowel.)

But I think that women on the prowl have spoiled the gentle sport, and every ship is full of them looking for the single men who aren't there, or who have better prospects in port. And how is a poor man to know these days whether flirtation is a game without a goal or a strategy for life? The acquisitive intensity of American women who interpret a gallant compliment as a proposal of marriage is not only the dismay of European men but possibly the greatest single inhibitor of the instinct towards flirtation in all the men she meets.

So much for boats. As for rolling stock, since the American train has given up providing even the minimal comforts, it can hardly be expected to service flirtation. Men use parlor cars to catch up on work and bar cars to catch up on drink, and as for the dining car, eyes that are riveted on lurching coffee are hardly free to drown in the gaze of others. Besides, who rides in trains these days except commuters or those grounded by weather —hardly amorous conditions?

And what of the airplane? Having sat in a window seat for thousands of miles over this glorious land, I can only testify that

For Husbands and Lovers

the neighboring seat is occupied by a woman or not at all. Nothing seems to strike terror in the American male like a seat next to a female: he will avoid it at all costs. Why? Because he thinks he will be talked at, and because he finds the talk of most women deadly. This I understand, with a certain sympathy. For in a plane he is stuck for the duration; he can not move away. And the tragedy is that the faster we go, the more we are trapped. In the older and slower planes of the past—the Flying Boat of the forties, the Stratocruiser of the early fifties—there were places for meeting and ways to change seats, and I remember, wistfully, several trips across the sea when the company of strange men provided exhilaration without risk.

But now there is nothing but the sterile seat plan of the jet-borne capsule and the cowardice of men who will not trade the *Reader's Digest* or *Business Week* for the brief knowledge of a strange woman. Who knows, she might be even more fun?

At this point, I am forced to admit that the average American male air traveler rarely compels curiosity. He is rather grey, inside and out, and he wears his clothes and his hat without any masculine dash. They are coverings, not statements. If he is old, his face is either hard-bitten or baby-soft; and if he is younger, he has no definite face at all: rather, an arrangement of features blurred to anonymity by adjustment. What's more, such men never look at a woman directly, although they study measurements. Such is our culture, in fact, that woman is not the sum of her dimensions, but her dimensions are the sum of woman. The nature of woman, the mind of woman, the spirit of woman— these, to most of our men, are irrelevancies. And when only the attributes of physical youth are able to arouse interest in a man, the value of a woman at any age lies undiscovered. Mature men know this. Grown-up adolescents don't. And it is they who form the enormous market for sex magazines, art stills, and girls for whom no preliminaries are required.

Now let me quickly, before an army of men protest, distribute blame equally for the decline of flirtation. Men and women make each other what they are; and if I have been concentrating on the conspicuous lack of masculine skill at this sport, or even engagement in it, it is because I am, so to speak, on the other side.

But I have observed enough to understand our share of the guilt and attempt to define it. The faces of most women on the street (literally speaking) hardly invite the gentler male approach. They are set, self-preoccupied, and cold-eyed. In fact, they seldom bother to look a man in the eye with that pleased appraisal that makes the passage of a man in the streets of Europe an adventure. And I am not speaking of professional appraisal.

Too many women either have no time to acknowledge the courtesies too few men pay them—opening doors, offering seats, picking things up—or assume that they are passes to be repulsed. It is the rare man who continues to suffer such bruises.

At parties, too few women accord the men they meet their whole attention. Either their gaze wanders, or their conversation is a monologue directed largely at themselves. Junior's school triumphs or the importance of World Federalism do not kindle the opposite eye. Nor does that narcissism, widely prevalent, that makes a woman more concerned with how she looks than with the man who is looking at her.

For the function of flirtation is to bring the illusion of intimacy to a public encounter; to warm, to amuse, to titillate, even to excite. It is a graceful salute to sex, a small impermanent spark between one human being and another, between a man and a woman not in need of fire. And it would make this impermanent life a lot more fun if more of us learned the art of keeping the spark alive, and glowing.

THE SOPHISTICATED
MAN

IF I SAID that the sophisticated man was what the sophisticated woman wanted, I would be begging trouble. Many a simple girl has yearned for a worldly lover, and many a complicated and polished woman has rushed into the arms of a simple brute. Perhaps I should say that I can remember no time in my life when the sophisticated man was not the object of my interest, if not my search. Unlike some women, I have never had the patience of an educator nor the zeal of a reformer. I prefer the finished product; not a man incapable of growth, but one who has managed to acquire those perceptions, tastes, and attitudes which, to me, constitute sophistication.

What was my yardstick? Well, in younger days when I traveled alone a great deal and had to develop certain techniques against unwanted aggressions, my preliminary judgments were largely visual. If I were standing in the corridor of a wagon-lits, for instance, and saw with the tail of my eye that a male was bearing down on me, I would retreat if he wore any of these things: a pale cloth cap, basket-weave sport shoes, and an ordinary shirt unbuttoned at the neck and exposing, usually, a bristling sprout of hair. These were the days, I am constrained to admit, before what is known as "casual" wear. Now my list of repellents—academically speaking—has formidably increased. It includes plastic raincovers on hats (I have seen them even on Shriner fezzes), jackets pulled down at the shoulder by the straps of heavy cameras, and the pale loose suits, pale hats, and pale ties which

73

mark the American male in all the hotel lobbies, streets, and airports across the country. On the beaches of the North in summer and the South in winter, I would beat a hasty withdrawal from men in matching patterned shorts and jackets or silly hats. And in bucolic parties alfresco, the fellow barbecuing in an apron printed with "Cordon Bleu" or "I Wear the Pants" will have to look elsewhere (which he usually does) for a female companion. I mention these trivialities of attire because I am convinced that the sophisticated man wouldn't be seen dead in them. They are, one and all, emasculators, and if there is anything which the worldly man cossets it is his male dignity. The bareheaded fellow in the khaki shorts and the dark-blue polo shirt has been around.

Now, here we come to the crux of the situation, for I maintain that a man who has never traveled in other countries and been exposed to other societies cannot be sophisticated. I am not speaking of package tours or cruise trips, but of a reasonable familiarity with foreign cities and peoples and arts and customs; an education reading alone cannot provide. For sophistication to me suggests, primarily, a refinement of the senses. The eye that has not appreciated Michelangelo's David in Florence or the cathedral of Chartres is not a sophisticated eye; nor is the tongue that has not tasted the best fettucine in Rome or the best wine in Paris. The hand that has not felt the rough heat of an ancient wall in Siena or the sweating cold of a Salzburg stein of beer is an innocent hand. So are the fingers that have not traveled, in conscious and specific savoring, over the contours of many different women.

Would you recognize this kind of man if you saw him across the room? I think so. He's the one talking with an attractive woman; conservatively dressed, but easy in his clothes. His hair is trimmed close to his head, but not too close. His hands are well-groomed, but not manicured. He does not laugh loudly or often. He is looking directly at the woman he speaks to, but he is not missing the other attractive women as they enter; a flick of the eye does it. For in all ways this man is not obvious. He would no more appear to examine a woman from the ankles up than he would move his head as he read or form the words with his lips. His senses are trained and his reflexes quick. And how did they get that way? From experience, from observation, and from deduction. He puts two and two together without adding on his fingers. He is educated in life.

Now what about that fellow over there—the one in the light-grey suit and the crew cut? He is telling a long story rather loudly to a girl who would rather not be hearing it. He is not, of course, aware of this, since he is not only a little tight but unaccustomed to watching the reactions of women. He will look down the front of her dress but not see the glaze on her eyes. He has not been educated in observation. He is, according to the dictionary, un-sophisticated in that he is natural and simple and lacking in experience. And this, again according to the dictionary, is a com-pliment. For the sophisticated are not only said to be refined to the point of artificiality, but might well—because of this, and in spite of their cleverness—be unsound.

Now Mr. Webster derived his definition from "sophism," which is clearly unpleasant in the company it keeps with fallacy and deceptive reasoning. But Mr. Webster was also an American, and it is no accident that his countrymen have for a long time shared the suspicion that sophisticated people—male or female—were somehow un-American. Open spaces and open people: that's what we've prided ourselves on. The good fellow, the regular guys, the gladhanders, no nonsense about 'em, you know just where they stand; they look you in the eye and talk straight; simple—natural—unaffected. And as for sophisticated women—they're all right for a laugh or a show or a week end, but who would want to marry 'em? No sir, give me the girl next door every time, like home-baked pie.

Sophistication, then, has always seemed something of an im-port, either from Europe or secondhand from New York. And when women think of sophisticated men, their minds wander from British diplomats to French actors to Italian princes, settling in the end for those American men—mostly in movies—who have made love to British duchesses, French models, or Italian actresses. If examples were wanted, Cary Grant and Henry Fonda would do quite nicely as dream images of the sophisticated male. Most of us, of course, do not meet Cary Grant or Henry Fonda. But we do travel, increasingly. And I would like to issue a warning to those of my countrywomen tempted to believe that a well-cut suit and a well-kept accent can transport them from Crestwood to the world of true values.

Some years ago there was a late-night television program on a local channel called "The Continental." On this a man oozing charm from every pore oiled his way not across the floor but into the hearts, apparently, of thousands of yearning housewives. He did this by looking straight into the camera eye as if it were yours, by raising a glass of wine, to you, of course, and, in an accent drenched with sauce marinara, murmuring sweet nothings of life and love to his unseen, but presumably panting, mistress. Ridiculed as he was by critics and confident husbands, the female response alarmed the sponsors into taking it off. It was not obscene, merely indecent.

Now I am not implying that continentals resemble this man. But they do possess a surface sophistication which may seem like the real thing even when it isn't. Their shirts are of the finest silk, their shoes handmade, and their hair of the proper length. They kiss your hand with the proper lightness, look into your eyes just long enough to create surface tension, their voices are well-modulated, and they do not rush you. They make a flattering show of savoring your intelligence, arriving at your body only at the dessert course of your first meal together. It is then that the tricks begin to show—to anyone, that is, not overcome by Soave and long black lashes. They employ a standard routine which is, precisely because it does not discriminate between you and a hundred other women, the product not of sophistication but of guile. It goes something like this: "You are beautiful, but you have not lived. Let me wake you. Only I can wake you. Most men want to take pleasure—I want to give it." Another very successful variation is the following gambit. The continental: "How can you be so beautiful and so cold!" Mary Jane from Wilmington: "I'm *not* cold!" The continental, whispering, breathing hard: "Then prove it to me!"

If you prove it to him, you may have some pleasurable moments, but you will discover before long that your Awakener is no more educated in world culture and the refinements of living than the agency man you met in Detroit, and probably less so. He may very well be a haberdasher who has never been out of Italy, thinks all Americans are rich, and lives in a room full of chromos and potted plants. Or he may be a Brazilian cocoa merchant who thinks all American men are uncultured and all American women are hard. These are the common men, adopting a veneer of worldliness that passes for sophistication. They have as I said, picked up some useful techniques. They know that specific flattery—"Your neck is like a column"—is more potent than general flattery—"You look swell"; that the ardent look can be more effective than the hasty grab; and that masculine self-assurance is the best weapon against feminine resistance. They know that a part of this assurance comes from good grooming and correct attire. But they are stereotypes for all that, while the mark of true sophistication is the absence of label.

As for our home-grown stereotypes, their approaches differ only in the crudity of their application and the fact that too often they are impelled by liquor. I have never considered the amorous lurch a compliment, nor the mumbled repetition of certain endearments accompanied by uncertain groping. I am bored by a man so simple, or so unsure, that he can approach a woman only by the chemical solvence of his inhibitions. I am dismayed by a man so unreticent that he can tell me about his wife and himself at our first encounter. This guilelessness, which is considered an American virtue, I find, as a woman, not only dull but immature. Reticence and sophistication go hand in hand, for one of the joys of life is discovery: the gradual peeling of layers. It is a pity, in fact, that the democratization of society has accelerated this process to the degree of Instant Intimacy, or Instimacy. Instead of a relished progression from *vous* to *tu*, from Mister to Jim, it's darling and come to my place in the first hour. Like many time-savers, small pleasures are sacrificed: you travel fast, but you miss the flowers on the roadside. And when you get there, what do you remember of the trip?

No. My sophisticated man does not tip his hand too soon; he savors the moves of the game, and only urgent reasons impel him to quick disclosure.

Now you must have gathered from the foregoing that the S.M. likes women. I would go further and say that he prefers the company of women to men. He is not one for conventions, evenings with the boys, or that postprandial segregation of the sexes still practiced by hostesses at the peril of their parties. This does not mean that he does not relish conversations with men, but that given a social choice he will favor the inclusion of women.

I have in my life met men of true sophistication in all other spheres who were still naïve in their judgments of women or diffident in their approaches to them. This could be attributed to their mothers, their endocrine balances, a childhood shock, or any one of those causative factors which explain everything and nothing. These are the men who fall in love with maternal women or childish women to avoid the challenge of their equals; or who, in their innocence, cannot discern between the generous woman and the promiscuous one until they are cuckolded. But then, have we not already discussed the men who show sophistication in their treatment of women, but little in other areas? Few of us, men or women, are of the same grain all the way through. Indeed, consistency would discourage that appetite for experience which is the basis of sophistication.

It would seem at first glance that this appetite would make the S.M. less moral than our natural, open, simple man. Again we return to the root of the old American-puritan distrust of him. Yet I maintain that the fine, upstanding, regular, all-American male who married the girl next door and likes steak more than gigot is really no more virtuous; he is merely less fastidious. It is he, on his business trips, who patronizes call girls. The sophisticated man can gratify his desires without paying for them. It is our unsophisticated big shot who uses his secretaries for more than typing; the wiser fellow keeps business and pleasure separate. It is our simple fellow who gets drunk at conventions and paws the high school drum majorette. Our complex man wouldn't be seen dead with her. The difference is that our regular guy has to prove his virility, while our sophisticated fellow quietly exercises it. He has long since abandoned proving for enjoying.

His enjoyments, as the full use of his senses would indicate, cover a wide range. How a man lives, what he surrounds himself with, is index enough of his sophistication, or lack of it, and there is nothing more revealing than a quiet prowl around his quarters. (I refer, of course, to bachelor quarters; a wife's contributions would complicate the issue.) Does he have flying geese over his mantel and the *Reader's Digest* on his coffee table? Does the one bookshelf in the room feature the works of Harold Robbins, Allen Drury, and *How to Make Two Million Dollars in Real Estate?* Does his record cabinet bulge with Kostelanetz and Gould, but lack Vivaldi or Bach or Fauré or Prokofiev? Then prepare for a simple man and a limited one. His heart may be gold, but his company will be leaden.

I suspect, moreover, the too-neat room, for it can imply a certain barrenness. The sophisticated man has many passions, and I salute them in the two-foot pile of magazines on his desk which can range from *The Listener* to the *Bulletin of Atomic Scientists* or in the unframed prints, abstract or classical, stacked on available ledges against the wall, awaiting hanging. I am also comforted by the presence in his kitchenette of hunks of cheese, some fruit, and a round loaf of bread, if nothing else. I suspect that his medicine cabinet may be rather full, for the price of sophistication is an awareness so constantly acute that it must be blunted from time to time. I would rather see a collection of pills, in short, than a rowing device.

If I am omitting the lair, or pad, of the beatnik, it is because I would not have gone to it in the first place; this exploration is for the very young. Odd as it may sound, the bearded Zen seeker and café poet is no more sophisticated than the glad-handing Shriner. He is merely less organized. They both abide by the conventions of their groups, their horizons equally limited. In the hygienic cheeriness of the Crestview home and the dirty clutter of the beatnik refuge there is the same sterility, the same exclusion of experience. There is in both the self-consciousness of the insecure. They live as they think they should. And it is not, thank heaven, with me.

As revealing as his rooms are the presents a man gives. Like most women I am grateful when anybody gives me anything, but my gratitude increases in direct relation to a man's selectivity. I love cashmere sweaters, but I naturally prefer one in a color that shows the donor's awareness of my own. I love jewels, but I am happier with a handsome piece of junk, that shows not only an appreciation of fashion but of *my* particular fashion, than I would be by a genuine jewel bearing no relation to it. I love perfume but I love it that much more when I know the giver has arrived at his choice after due trial.

I suspect that many of my countrywomen and more of my countrymen may find in my S.M. the portrait of an urban monster —effete, affected, immoral, snobbish, and unreliable. Urbane he certainly is, although I would put an appreciation of the natural world high in his category of perceptions. The man unaware or unmoved by the sea or the sky or the rock or the stream or the flower is not sophisticated; he is merely half-alive. As for the imputed defects, I do not hold them as such. Instead of effete, I would say civilized; instead of affected, effective; instead of immoral, curious; instead of snobbish, superior.

As for unreliable, the sophisticated husband is more aware of the hazards and inconveniences of infidelity than the innocent one, if only because he has been married before.

Some years ago at a large party I met a man whose reputation had preceded him as a brilliant writer and the contented husband of a handsome wife. After fifteen minutes of spirited but impersonal conversation, he took my hand and said very quietly, "I love you." He knew that I knew that he meant it. I knew that he would never leave his wife. We shared a mutual knowledge, separately arrived at.

And that, I think, is the final virtue of sophistication. It is a condition beyond explanation.

THE NEW UPPER CLASS, THE KIDS

THE CASE for the Prosecution wishes to submit the following evidence for the jury's consideration:

Exhibit 1: A television commercial advertising a polyunsaturated product in which a father and two children are seated at a table. As the mother brings in a heaping platter of hot food, the children shout, "Aw gee, Ma, we wanted fried chicken!"

Exhibit 2: Another commercial in which a boy on his bicycle swerves into a flower bed. The returning commuter-father snaps at him. ("Why take it out on those you love?")

Exhibit 3: A third commercial in which children mess up walls, furniture, and floors with muddy hands and feet and Mom cleans up delightedly with a new detergent.

Before producing further evidence of the exalted status of the defendant, Child, and the corollary subjugation of the adult, let us examine these exhibits more closely. In exhibit 1, it is further shown that the mother accedes to the wishes of the young and turns out the fried chicken, instead, as minimal sense would dictate, of telling them to shut up and eat what's there.

In exhibit 2, the father has every right to snap at a boy for driving over the flower bed when there are ample pathways at hand. Instead, he blames his irritation on his stomach, takes a pill, and buddies up to the boy.

In exhibit 3, the state concedes that children get dirty but submits that if they persist in transferring this condition to their parents' abode, they be made to clean up their own mess.

We would like, furthermore, to call to the jury's attention the fact that these commercials are seen by millions and that they presumably reflect common experiences and attitudes in this country.

Further evidence abounds of the inordinate power exerted by our young, of the child orientation existing in our society for the last decades, and of the abdication of parents, out of fear and intimidation, from their rightful and normal functions as decision makers.

I should like to call my first witness. Mrs. Williams, you were in the Beauty Queen Beauty Salon on the tenth of this month, were you not?

I was.

Would you tell in your own words what you saw there?

Well, I was having my hair set next to a little girl of about ten, who was having a comb-out—you know, teased and all.

Yes, go on.

Well, she was telling the woman stylist how to do it, and she said, "It oughta be higher here and fuller there, so it's kinda softer on the face."

You actually heard those words, Mrs. Williams?

Yes, sir, I did. And her mother was sitting right close having a manicure and she said, "Isn't she a riot?"

Thank you, Mrs. Williams. I would like to call my next witness. Mrs. Jones, you are the mother of five, are you not?

Yes, sir.

Would you tell the jury how you make family decisions?

For Husbands and Lovers

Well, we believe in democracy, you see, and before we decide anything—

What is anything, Mrs. Jones?

Oh, you know, what to buy, where to go for vacation, that sort of thing.

Thank you. Please go on.

Well, we have a meeting. Petey—he's six—was the chairman last time. My husband and I wanted to go to the mountains this summer—he likes to hike and fish, that sort of thing—but the kids wanted the seashore.

So what happened then, Mrs. Jones?

Well, they were in the majority, so we went to the beach. My husband got awful burned.

Thank you, Mrs. Jones.

Ladies and gentlemen of the jury, I could keep you here far into the night with a parade of witnesses testifying to similar episodes and practices. Or I could quote you a sheaf of clippings like the two I have here in my hand. One is from a Nassau County judge who deplores what he calls the serious malady of automania in suburban youth. "I am seriously disturbed," he says, "by the number of teen-agers . . . who feel they just can't live without a car and who are stealing cars, or going for joy rides without permission, or showboating in cars to such an extent that their vehicle becomes a deadly weapon." The judge cited the case of a teen-ager who said he was "mad at the world" because he did not own a car, stole one, and drove over the fences and lawns of twenty-five homes.

Another clipping is from that genial observer of American life, Harry Golden. Speaking of our child-oriented culture, he wrote: "When the police chief starts banning all the paperbacks which deal with sex, his reason is always that such and such a book or books will corrupt and contaminate children. The largest volume of outrage I've ever heard mustered occurred one Christmas season when the local movie booked a Brigitte Bardot instead of the usual animal film over the holidays."

But Will It Sell?

I would like to summarize the main points of the Prosecution's case, based on prolonged study by qualified observers:

The causes which led to children becoming the "take-over generation"—a phrase used by *Life* in reference to hard-eyed young men—are several. One was a loose interpretation of the Freudian dogma that a word spoken harshly to a child of three would warp him at twenty. Another was the assumption that every little being has something to express and must therefore be free to express it. A third was the astounding theory that children were adults and should be treated as such.

Add to these certain educational tenets to the effect that learning must not only be made easy but entertaining, that no child must be pushed, and that, on the contrary, he must proceed according to his own rate of development, and it is small wonder that there has grown up in this nation a vast and powerful pressure group of children and teen-agers who have come to dictate the terms of the life not only which *they* lead but which, perforce, their parents must also accept.

These same parents are only beginning to realize—and rebel against—the extent of this domination. They are at last aware that the records they hear, the shows they see on television, the cars they buy, and the colleges they pay for are less their choice than the dictation of their young, now crew-cut or draped-hair or bee-hived teen-agers. The wails played by disk jockeys, the pornography sold with comic books, the soft drinks and candies that rot their teeth, are aimed at young ears, young eyes, and young mouths devoid of discrimination: the children the parents allowed to take over.

For the parents alone are not to blame. Their children acquired powerful allies in the sellers of goods, who discovered this marvellous new market of youth some time ago. They planned an infinite variety of methods to remove the weekly allowance and earnings of America's young ones, which in aggregate amounts to nearly ten billion dollars a year. From the age of four onwards, the juvenile consumer is bombarded with messages to buy.

As for the older child, the strange cult of the teen-ager is the natural result of this early consumer training. This young human being is led to believe that once he becomes thirteen he becomes a member of the superior race. What the teen-ager does, wears, wants, and thinks is considered of such prime importance that it must be catered to not only by the outside world but inside the home. The beleaguered parents suddenly find themselves confronted by a dominant and usually hostile herd who take over the house, the meals, the TV set, and the conversation. The adults are unwanted guests in their own home.

Parents are also the victims of a pattern of life which removes one potential controlling factor for ten hours a day for five days a week: the father. His absence (unmourned, we suspect, by him) leaves the care of the young entirely to a mother distracted by the proliferating duties imposed by laborsaving devices. Between the whir of the dishwasher, the ring of the telephone, and the roar of the vacuum cleaner, she has found it less and less possible to control the large brood she had been steadily increasing since her marriage at eighteen. The easiest thing was to send them out on the communal lawn to play with the other savages, or let their shrilling ranks be stilled by machine-gun fire from the television set. She was, in any case, outnumbered. As for Dad after a tough business day, it took all his remaining energy to make his voice heard at meals over the *musique concrète* of their massed clamor. Abdication was easier.

The distinguished author Henry James viewed this domination with alarm in 1882—eighty-one years ago, ladies and gentlemen. In "The Point of View," he wrote: ". . . the young people are eating us up—there is nothing in America but the young people. The country is made for the rising generation; life is arranged for them; they are the destruction of society. People talk of them, consider them, defer to them, bow down to them. They are always present, and whenever they are present there is an end to everything else. . . . But the little boys kick your shins, and the little girls offer to slap your face! There is an immense literature entirely addressed to them, in which the kicking of shins and the slapping of faces are much recommended. . . . The future is theirs;

maturity will evidently be at an increasing discount. Longfellow wrote a charming little poem, called 'The Children's Hour,' but he ought to have called it 'The Children's Century.' And by children, of course, I don't mean simple infants; I mean everything of less than twenty."

Like all great artists, Mr. James was a prophet. But even he did not envisage a time when adults actually became afraid of their young. Those of you who walk the streets of any city or town, who use public transit or visit public parks have reason to be. We are not speaking here of gangs, although they are an extreme form of this tyranny: the outcome not of parental indulgence but of parental neglect. We are concerned rather with the general aspect of the young at large: the slouching poor-complexioned boys with greased long hair in elaborate waves and insolent walk; the hard-eyed hussies of girls decked out in the advertised trappings of sex. Both use words of violent sexual vulgarity.

You say, ladies and gentlemen, that your young are not like this? Maybe not. In the fashionable suburbs, in the private schools, on selective campuses across the nation you may find the clear-eyed, mannerly, intelligent young folk on whom the future good of our nation resides. The Prosecution claims that they are a minority and that the majority—the roamers of streets, the gatherers at street corners, the loungers on steps—are a destructive force against the fabric of our society by virtue or evil of their inflated importance. In their precocious claim to adult status, in their premature worldliness, they have lost the innocence which is not only the child's birthright but prime requisite for basic rectitude.

Now I am sure I can anticipate the summation for the Defense of the Child as Master. My distinguished antagonist will use the word "freedom" lavishly. The child must be free to grow. The child must be free to express himself. The child must be free to be free. And the Defense will doubtless cite the grievous psychic wounds inflicted by discipline, by denial, by parental ukase of any sort.

The Defense, if I may say so, is behind the times. For there is a revolt brewing. To a growing number of adults, the reign of the child and teen-ager has become insupportable and hence near termination.

What is more, there is a distinct lack of evidence that the young who have been catered to in every way grow up to be better or more mature or productive adults than their less-favored elders. Distinguished psychologists, in fact, are now beginning to question whether the objects of continual maternal attention and day-long presence are better off than children brought up partly by others, or for that matter, in the well-staffed day nurseries used in other civilized societies.

That distinguished American citizen Winston Churchill was, like many great persons, reared to a large extent by governesses and tutors; vanished breeds, to be sure, but an indication that mothers are not necessarily always best fitted to raise their own.

There is one more point, in conclusion, which the Prosecution finds it pertinent to raise. It is simply this: that parents are being outnumbered. In their indulgence of large families they have reaped their own whirlwind; or to be more literal, contributed to an imbalance of nature for which not only they, but future generations will pay. The child has become father to the man.

It is the Prosecution's intention to reverse this condition. I ask you now, therefore, ladies and gentlemen of the jury, to return a verdict of guilty against the defendant.

It is for the Judge, of course, to deliver the sentence. Yet irregular as it is for the Prosecution to do so, we submit a few suggestions for the rehabilitation of the young defendant:

From the ages of four to twelve, all decisions concerning diet, clothing, household products, vacations, television, movies, schools, and reading are to be made by the parents without consultation with the young.

From the ages of twelve to sixteen, the same decisions are to be made by the parents after consultation, but not necessarily in agreement with the young.

No teen-ager under eighteen is permitted to own a car or to use the family car except in cases of emergency. Defendant is to walk or take public transit for all other purposes, including dating.

Defendant is to rise when adults come into the room and leave it when adults ask him to. The destruction of adult conversation by childish chatter is an act of sabotage punishable by expulsion.

Girls are to be forbidden cosmetic aids or professional hair care until the age of sixteen, and then only for special social occasions.

If by no other virtue than superior age and experience, the adult is to be reinstated to his rightful position of importance in the family, the community, and the nation.

The Prosecution finally suggests that the verdict of guilty be accompanied by a recommendation for mercy. The Prosecution has four delightful children who will otherwise lynch him when he gets home.

3: *The Violent Society*

PREFACE

<hr/>

BANG-BANG-BANG! POW! ACK-ACK-ACK-ACK-ACK!

How many times have you seen a child crouching in ambush, forefinger pointing or toy gun barrel raised as the gleeful voice parrots the ping of the bullet or the chatter of the machine gun? How many times have you bought them these guns or let them sit long hours before a small screen watching men draw and sight and pull, and other men clutch their sides as they fall off horses or sprawl on the pavements, dead? And have you ever been in a local movie theatre on a Saturday afternoon and heard the children who fill it shriek with laughter as guerilla forces in some old war film slaughter the enemy with machine-gun fire? Or overheard roving adolescents (not yours, of course, although they might be) spit obscenities at each other instead of words?

But Will It Sell?

You may see no connection between such things and the murder of the President of the United States. But some people have. One of them, Walter Lippmann, wrote this five days after the unspeakable crime:

"The divisive forces of hatred and ungovernability are strong among us, and the habit of intemperate speech and thought has become deeply ingrained. It is deepened by the strains of war and the frustrations of this revolutionary age, by the exploitation of violence and cruelty in the mass media, by the profusion of weapons and by the presence of so many who know how to use them."

Lippmann is saying here what many of us have known for a long time: that there is a climate of violence in this country that threatens its strength, its unity, and its security more than any external danger.

The pattern is not confined to any one part of the nation or any one kind of person. Violence shamed Little Rock before the world seven years ago, and Birmingham last year: the murder of Medgar Evers, the bombing of little girls in an Alabama church, were monstrous sins against humanity. In Dallas three years ago, the man who is now our President was spat upon and cursed by a seething mob in a hotel lobby, and only months ago a Dallas youth spat in the face of the United States Ambassador to the United Nations and a woman hit his head with a picket sign. In New York, pickets jostled, jeered at, and threatened the Chief Justice of the United States Supreme Court. In the South and in the North, white boys and white mothers screamed —and scream—at Negro children going to school and at Negro adults moving into a white development. North and South and East and West, middle-class and upper-class white men and women who call themselves conservative pledge an allegiance of hate against persons or bodies dedicated to the enlightenment of man, the alleviation of his burdens, and the preservation of peace through world order. Under the banner of patriotism and anti-Communism, they give themselves license for violence in word and deed against the very constitutional principles which they claim to preserve. And in supposedly civilized social circles, men and women of education and substance made the late President of the United States an object of ridicule, scorn, profanity, belittlement, and outright hatred.

And while the adults of the nation thus give the cue for such "intemperate speech and thought," the young—white and colored, North and South and East and West—steal, rape, kill, peddle dope, or commit vandalism in a paroxysm of rage against, or profound boredom with, the world around them. Not a day passes without some story of a boy who shoots his parents because they asked him to do his homework, or of packs of youths who stomp or shoot a man dead because he had only twenty cents in his pocket and they wanted more.

These people—these haters and these attackers and killers—are not a majority; but they are a minority too threatening to ignore and too large for a healthy society to absorb without infinite harm to itself.

How did they get that way? The litany of reasons is familiar enough: ignorance, poverty, discrimination, prejudice, war generation, rootlessness, science, the bomb, the cold war, unemployment, housing, and so forth. For over a decade some have wondered out loud whether the diet of violence fed the nation's children through mass media did not bear a large part of the responsibility, but these have usually been disposed of with the epithet of "zealot" and reminded that the mass media could indeed be a contributory factor in the case of those already unstable and disturbed, but in general—and conversely—have helped children to "sublimate their aggressive instincts" and left the healthy unaffected.

In spite of these soothing rationalizations on the part of child-guidance specialists, poll takers, sociologists, broadcasters, and comic-book publishers, the zealots kicked up enough dust to cause a diminution in television horror shows and the elimination of the most sadistic comic books. Yet any close examination of television programming still reveals a daily parade of crime, violence, and murder; and any perusal of comic books shows, at the very least, a perversion of values and a dependence on fist, gun, and verbal threat to convey their "entertainment."

And most especially, the gun. One wonders if the drafters of the Second Amendment of our Constitution, permitting citizens to bear arms in their own defense, could have possibly envisaged that two hundred years later any American youth could buy a gun without a license or reference in any American city, and that the weapon which killed the President of the United States was bought through the mails for twelve dollars and seventy-eight cents.

Thus does the gun—the great equalizer—make it possible for a weak and miserable man to exercise the power of death over a great and strong one.

Violence as a way to power, force as a solution to problems: these are the crutches of all the confused and weak. Bomb the church; hose the "niggers"; impeach the Chief Justice; kick out the U.N.; drop the Bomb; invade Cuba; "kill the bastard!" The people who say and think these things are not far removed from Lee Oswald and Jack Ruby. They believe in force rather than reason, they have contempt for the rule of law, they are taking justice into their own hands. They have no faith in the mind and spirit of man which sets him above animals or in the institutions which are testimonials to his vision.

And the young hear what they say. They hear their fathers call the Supreme Court communist and the President a four-letter word. They overhear the sly sniggers and dirty jokes of Americans who consider as enemies, inferiors, and traitors all those who think differently from themselves. They are confronted daily by people who have no control over their emotions, no rein on their prejudices, no respect for their fellows. They see wherever they go how law is flouted and reason trampled.

But these are not the only manifestations of a common violence that has afflicted this nation and that was given terrible focus by the crime in Dallas. Mass-produced pornography is a form of violence: an expression of contempt of woman which makes her nothing more than the object of an impersonal lust and the instrument only of erotic gratification, both violent in their compulsion. Millions of dollars are made in this country by the flood of pornography and sadism to which every school child has access. The men responsible for this wholesale pollution are protected by our constitutional right to freedom of speech and by our healthy evasion of any censorship which might abridge it. With staggering cynicism they defend their "rights" against even the most tentative efforts to establish a difference—with a view towards control—between the violence-sex-sadism which is clearly packaged for commercial ends only and the eroticism or violence which a serious and talented writer may not be able to divorce from his material without damaging his vision of truth. The result is the tacit sanction of wholesale filth in the name not only of freedom of speech but of free enterprise. Confronted with a choice between a sickening of the social tissues and a curtailment of profits, we prefer to accept the former on the grounds that it is not really provable.

Against such realities, and the continuing evidence of them in your daily papers, it is not enough to say that healthy people are not affected by such inducements to violence. The truth of the matter is that far too many Americans are sick in mind and in spirit. On the very night that the President of the United States was murdered in Dallas, the cranks and the haters continued to foul the air. The assistant chief of detectives in Washington said that the authorities there had received threatening telephone calls against "virtually every dignitary here." The time has come in friendly, free America when the leaders of a democracy must be guarded against their own people.

What then can we do, not to achieve a security which cannot ever be wholly attained, but to return to a climate of reason, sanity, and respect without which no free society can long survive?

We will have to start by building up within ourselves a forbearance and control which outlaws intemperate words and deeds no matter how much we differ from others, no matter how strongly we feel. With this example or responsibility, the young may grow to contain their aggressive forces or, better, channel them into productive outlets. Their violence has a great deal to do with idleness, boredom, and lack of direction, and we had better examine very closely what it is in our way of living that produces this vacuum.

Practically, legislation should be passed to make the distribution and sale of weapons illegal except through a stringent procedure of licensing that weeds out or at least sharply diminishes the number of buyers without specific and provable need for the possession of a gun. That this might infringe on the sportsman's rights is of concern only to those who think the sport of shooting animals is more important than the means to prevent the slaughter of citizens.

As for violence on the mass media, the fable, "The Conquest of Trigger Mortis," which appears later in this section, suggests one step towards the total disarmament of the American child, if not of his world.

Difficult as it may be, a definition of mass pornography must be arrived at in order for its distribution to be made an indictable offense, with enforcement promptly imposed.

If some such action is not ultimately taken, none of us can depend on the laws which hoped to offer all of us life, liberty, and the pursuit of happiness.

DEAR MUMMY

Mrs. Howard Andrews
Our Place
Crestview, Ohio

Dear Addie,

Your father and I are very disturbed about something we just
heard from the Maitlands (they came aboard yesterday for
drinks). Ginny said that just before they left for Flat Key, Ann
Rossiter called her from Oakdale and said that the Westover girl
had given a birthday party that turned into something of a riot.
She was very vague about the details, but it seems things got
very rough and the house was a shambles. We are very worried
because we remembered that Doug had been seeing something
of the Westover girl, and we naturally hope he wasn't involved.
Please let us know what, if anything, happened.

Love,
Mummy

Mr. and Mrs. Curtis Munson
Fool's Paradise
Flat Key, Bahamas

Dearest Mummy,

It's just like Ginny Maitland to go gabbing away like that up-
setting people for no reason. We are all trying to keep the

97

affair in the family, so to speak, and Howie even saw to it that Ed Bates didn't print anything about it in the Oakdale Sentinel.

Franny Westover *did* give a birthday party for about a hundred kids, and I guess it went on a little late and the boys wanted some fun and threw a few things around. Doug doesn't seem to remember what exactly happened, he said they "twisted" and then someone thought it would be funny if they had a "book-wetting," so they took all the books in the house and threw them in the swimming pool, and then someone else (I think it was a girl) thought it would be fun to have everyone take off their ordinary clothes and dress in window curtains. Dick Westover was very unpleasant over the phone yesterday (we never liked him anyway) and accused Doug of being one of the boys who cut up the living room rug with pruning shears, but it was a hideous mustard broadloom (that house is in the *worst* taste) and I don't much blame them.

The point is, Daddy, it was a simple case of high spirits and no real harm done. Just to smooth things over, I gave Doug a check for $300 to cover some glassware and the rug business (he swears he didn't burn any curtains).

So please don't worry about it, Doug is a fine boy, really, and those were the nicest kids anyone would want to know, all from the best homes and Yale and Princeton and all that.

Love and Kisses,
Addie

Mrs. Howard Andrews
Our Place
Crestview, Ohio

Dear Addie,

Your father had one of his indigestion attacks after getting your letter, and has asked me to write you.

The Violent Society

I need hardly say we were appalled. How is it possible for boys of decent families to destroy the property of other people who are giving them a party? And why weren't there any grownups at the party to stop them? In my days, the parents and older people were always around.

Your Distressed Mother,
Mother

P. S. If I'd been you and Howie I'd have made Doug pay for the damage out of his own pocket and taken away his college tuition for a semester. How else will these spoiled young ruffians ever learn?

Dad

Mrs. Curtis Munson
Fool's Paradise
Andros, Bahamas

Dear Mummy,

Your letter shows how out of touch you two have been with things today. No self-respecting parent would *dream* of being in the house when the kids are having a party, it inhibits them so. Howie and I just engage the band and the caterer and have our own fun somewhere else. Just to be on the safe side, we *did* hire a policeman for Carol's last party to see that the "crashers" didn't get too out of hand. In case you didn't know, it's the custom for a lot of kids to drive to a party they haven't been asked to, and in a way I think it's very democratic even if they do make a sort of mess of the place. But we always get a house-cleaning crew in the next day to sweep up the broken glass, refinish the furniture, and plant new bushes. It's just part of the expense of entertaining these days.

Also I don't see how you can say Doug is spoiled. He deserved a new Thunderbird for getting into Yale (Howie never thought he'd make it), and as for his speedboat this summer, you couldn't really expect him to take his dates across the lake in an outboard.

Doug is *not* a "ruffian." Why only the other day, Mr. Ballard (he's Vice President of Western Swivel) told Howie that Doug was a natural leader with a real feeling for money.

Love,
Addie

Mrs. Howard Andrews
Our Place
Crestview, Ohio

Dear Addie,

"Natural leaders with a real feeling for money" have been known to land in jail. Doug may too some day if you and Howie don't set him straight before it's too late.

Speaking of which, have you ever bothered to tell the kid about Right and Wrong and Responsibility? Where's his father been all this time? How can you possibly expect kids who drink hard liquor from fourteen on and crash parties and need policemen to keep them in order to turn into decent citizens?

High spirits my hat! Those boys need a flogging or a psychiatric examination. Not that I believe in that stuff, it's mostly mumbo-jumbo, but something must be wrong inside if a boy has to destroy something to feel good.

Love,
Dad

The Violent Society

Mrs. Curtis Munson
Fool's Paradise
Eleuthera, Bahamas

Dear Mummy,

I can't write to Dad in his present condition, he just doesn't understand the realities of today.

For one thing, Doug went to Sunday School from the ages of 8 to 10, and then at prep school they had the Lord's Prayer every morning before they banned it. So he's had as good a Christian upbringing as anyone.

For another, Dad seems to forget that when Doug was fifteen he won the D.A.R. prize for the best essay on Why Our Way of Life is the Best Way. So don't talk to me about ethics.

And what does Dad mean asking where Howie's been? Howie's in town every day as he well knows, working so that we can all have a decent standard of living, and it isn't his fault that he doesn't see his son from one end of the week to the other. It's the mother's responsibility anyway, and God knows I've given Doug everything since he was a tiny baby.

What Dad refuses to realize is that it's terribly hard growing up, with the bomb and insecurity and China, and boys like Doug don't know what's going to happen to them so they have to have some outlet somewhere.

Love,
Addie

Telegram to Mrs. Howard Andrews
RE OUTLET HOW ABOUT HONEST WORK OR THE PEACE CORPS?

Dad

But Will It Sell?

Mr. Curtis Munson
Fool's Paradise
St. James, Barbados

Dear Curtis,

Addie has just showed me your letter and telegram, and as she is rather emotional about all this, I thought I'd write to you directly.

My personal view is that the Communists were behind all these so-called riots you read about. I don't doubt that some Harvard red got into that Westover party and planted the whole thing so that it would reflect badly on our society.

Anyway, you have no cause to worry about Doug. He's a fine red-blooded kid with a great sense of humor and a lot of git-up-and-go.

What it all comes down to is, what would you rather have: a free society or a socialist state?

Cordially,
Howie

Miss Frances Westover
Oakdale, Ohio

Dear Fran,

I'm sorry you thought I sounded mad when you phoned me the news yesterday, but you can understand why it was something of a shock, especially as I don't remember a thing that happened that night, any more than you did. Somebody shot the lights out and I couldn't see who the hell I was with.

Honest, I'm really glad it was you and we might as well have a family now as later anyway.

I'll break the news to my old bag next weekend. It'll take her mind off this price-fixing and Dad's company you've probably read about.

Anyway, relax, I'll be calling you.

Your everlovin Doug

Mr. and Mrs. Curtis Munson
Fool's Paradise
Tobago, Trinidad

Dear Dad and Mom,

I know you'll be as happy as I am to know that Doug is engaged to Frances Westover and they hope to be married very soon. She's a darling girl (they're Mainland Steel), and they seem in a romantic daze about each other. So you see, the little Doug who worried you so is now about to be a responsible married man and, of course, some day, the father of a family.

I am hoping that after he finishes college (Howie naturally will see them through that), they'll settle somewhere near us so that the children can grow up in a fine healthy community with people who think alike and have the same values.

Doug will write you himself, I know. In spite of his sometimes casual manner, he is really very fond of you both, even if the generations don't always mix. Young people are more realistic, don't you think?

Lovingly,
Addie

THE CONQUEST OF
TRIGGER MORTIS

THE RULING was passed in 1970, over the total opposition of the TV and radio networks and after ten years of controversy, six investigations, 483 juvenile murders, and the complete reorganization of the Federal Communications Commission. What finally pushed it through was the discovery of *trigger mortis* in a number of American children born in widely separated areas. In this malformation the index finger is permanently hooked, forcing partial contraction of the whole hand in the position required for grasping a revolver. "The gun," said a distinguished anthropologist, "has become an extension of the American arm."

This mutation had been suspected some time before by others, who had found it worthy of note that in 1959, for instance, American toy manufacturers had sold more than $60 million worth of guns and revolvers and that on any given day on television between one and ten o'clock there were more than fifteen programs devoted to violence, and that in each of these programs a gun was fired at least once and usually several times. The only difference between the programs was that in some the shooting was done out of doors and often from horses and that in others it was done in hotel rooms, bars, or apartments. The first category was called Western and was considered a wholesome fight between good men and bad men in healthy country; the second was called Crime and Detective and was considered salubrious in its repeated implication that "crime does not pay," although the women and the interiors shown were usually expensive and the criminal's life, though short, a rich one.

Although this wholesale preoccupation with killing by gun coincided for many years with the highest rate of juvenile crime ever known in this country, and with open access to firearms for all who desired them, television and radio violence was considered by most experts of minimal importance as a contributory cause of youthful killing. Psychiatrists, social workers, program directors, advertisers, and sponsors had a handy set of arguments to prove their point. These (with translation appended) were the most popular:

❡ Delinquency is a complex problem. No single factor is responsible. (Don't let's stick our necks out. Don't let's act. Don't let's lose money.)

❡ It's all a matter of the home. (Blame the parents. Blame the neighborhood. Blame poverty.)

❡ Crime and adventure programs are a necessary outlet for natural childhood aggressions. (Keep the little bastards quiet while Mummy fixes supper.)

❡ We don't really know what influences children. (Let's wait till they kill somebody.)

❡ Only disturbed or abnormal children are affected by what they see on programs. (And they are a minority. Let their psychiatrists worry about them.)

Everybody was very pleased with these conclusions, particularly the broadcasters, who could continue presenting thirty shootings a day secure in those sections of their old printed Code, which stated: ". . . such subjects as violence and sex shall be presented without undue emphasis and only as required by plot development or character delineation"; and "Television shall exercise care in . . . avoiding material which is excessively violent or would create morbid suspense, or other undesirable reactions in children." These same officials continued also to exercise care in not letting their own children look at the programs of violence which they broadcast.

But Will It Sell?

So for years, and in spite of sporadic cries of alarm and protest from parents and a number of plain citizens, there were always enough experts to assure the public that crime and violence had nothing to do with crime and violence, and that gunplay was entertainment. Psychiatrists continued to say things like this about young killers: "The hostility, festering perhaps from the time he had been trained to the toilet, screamed for release," and educational groups came out periodically with reports on delinquency in which a suggested solution would be "to orient norm-violating individuals in the population towards a law-abiding lower-class way of life."

Dialogues like the following were frequent in Congressional investigations. This one occurred in a hearing of the Senate sub-committee on Juvenile Delinquency in 1954:

SENATOR: "In your opinion, what is the effect of these Western movies on children?"

EXPERT: "No one knows anything about it."

SENATOR: "Well, of course, you know that little children 6, 7, 8 years old now have belts with guns. Do you think that is due to the fact that they are seeing these Western movies and seeing all this shooting?"

EXPERT: "Oh, undoubtedly."

In the early 1950's, psychiatrist Fredric Wertham, from whose *The Circle of Guilt* the above was quoted, began a relentless campaign against what he called, in another book, *The Seduction of the Innocent*. Concentrating at first on horror and crime comics, the doctor moved inevitably into other fields of mass communication and provided impressive evidence along the way that although their gigantic dosage of violence could not be the sole factor in child criminality, it could certainly be considered a major one.

In attacking the slogan "It's all up to the home," he wrote: "Of course the home has a lot to do with it. But it is wrong to accuse the home as a cause in the usual abstract way, for the home is inseparable from other social circumstances to which it is itself vulnerable. . . . A hundred years ago the home could guard the children's safety; but with the new technological

advances, the modern parent cannot possibly carry this responsibility. We need traffic regulations, school buses, school zones,
and police to protect children from irresponsible drivers. Who
will guard the child today from irresponsible adults who sell him
incentives, blueprints, and weapons for delinquency?"

Wertham also countered the familiar claim that youthful violence was a result of wars by stating that it was not backed up
by any scientific, concrete study and that neither the Second
World War nor the Korean War explained the phenomenon:
". . . after the First World War the type of brutal violence cur-
rently committed on a large scale by the youngest children was
almost unknown."

But Wertham was dismissed by many of his colleagues and
much of the public as a man obsessed; too aggressively and
intemperately committed to one cause—the rape of children's
minds by mass communications—to be seriously considered. And
the broadcasters and crime-comic publishers, first needled and
exasperated by him, soon were able to view him with calm detachment as a crackpot. Thirty murders a day continued on the
screen.

Then, early in 1959, the Nuffield Foundation in England put
out a thick book called *Television and the Child,* by Hilde T.
Himmelweit, A. N. Oppenheim, and Pamela Vince. For four
years they examined thousands of children in five cities and of
every class and background, and to this they joined a survey of
American programming and viewing. They did not confine themselves to programming specifically for children, since it had long
been obvious in England, as it was here, that children usually
watched adult programs in preference. In more than four hundred pages of meticulous research, scientific detachment, and
careful reasoning, they came to certain conclusions—the basis
for a weight of further evidence that led, ten years later, to
government intervention into broadcasting practices. Here are a
few of their findings about the twenty per cent of programs seen
by children in their peak viewing hours that are devoted to
aggression and violence:

"At the center of preoccupation with violence is the gun.

But Will It Sell?

Everyone has a gun ready for immediate use—even the barbers and storekeepers, who are not cowboys. People in Westerns take guns for granted. . . . Finally, while guns are used mostly for killing, they are also let off for fun. Nevertheless, guns spell power, they make people listen, and force them to do what is wanted.

"It is said that these programmes have two main desirable effects: they teach the lesson that crime does not pay; and they provide a harmless outlet through fantasy for the child's hostile feelings. We shall take issue with both statements. . . . The lesson as taught in these programmes is entirely negative (it is best not to offend against the law). . . . To present such a one-sided view, repeated week after week, is contrary to the recognized educational principle that a moral lesson, to be effective, must teach what should be done as well as what should not be done.

"More serious is the fact that . . . the child may equally well learn other, less desirable lessons from these programmes; that to shoot, bully, and cheat is allowed, provided one is on the right side of the law; and that relationships among people are built not on loyalty and affection but on fear and domination. . . ."

As for being a "harmless outlet for aggressive feelings," the authors—quoting the testimony of Dr. Eleanor E. Maccoby of Harvard that this discharge in fantasy alters nothing in the child's real life and so has no lasting values—write that when aggressive feelings exist, "They are not as a rule discharged on viewing crime and violence." "We cite three sets of data . . . [which] show that aggressive feelings are just as likely to be aroused as to be lessened through viewing these programmes—indeed, this seems more often to be the case." And, quoting Dr. Maccoby again, ". . . the very children who are presumably using the movie as an outlet for their aggressive feelings are the ones who carry away the aggressive content in their memories, for how long we do not know."

Miss Himmelweit and her colleagues sum up as follows: "It is suggested that crime and violence programmes increase tension and anxiety, increase maladjustment and delinquent behaviour, teach children techniques of crime, blunt their sensitivity to suffering and, related to this, suggest to them that conflict is best solved by aggression.

"Our findings and those of Maccoby suggest, then, that these programmes do not initiate aggressive, maladjusted, or delinquent behaviour, but may aid its expression. They may not affect a stable child, but they may evoke a response in the 5-10 per cent of all children who are disturbed or at least emotionally labile, 'a group to be reckoned with by all the responsible people in the field of mass communications.'"

"We find . . . ," says the Nuffield Report, closing this chapter, "evidence that [these programs] may retard children's awareness of the serious consequences of violence in real life and may teach a greater acceptance of aggression as the normal, manly solution of conflict. . . . Just as a nation improves public hygiene when the evidence *suggests, without necessarily proving it* [my italics], that harm may otherwise result, so, we think, there is need of remedial action here."

The Nuffield Report authors had obviously fallen into the error of blaming the industry instead of the child. For in most "acceptable" studies of television and its influence, wrote Wertham, "the assumption seems to be that when anything goes wrong the child must be morbid but the entertainment normal. Why not assume . . . that our children are normal, that they like adventure and imagination, that they can be stimulated to excitement, but that maybe something is wrong with what they are looking at? Why assume that they need death and destruction . . . ?"

Voices, voices, voices. "Beefs," "squawks," the broadcasters called these surges of protest year after year. And they would point with pride to the one children's program out of ten that was educational, the one out of twenty that had no shooting.

But their biggest defense became, in the end, their undoing. They had assured themselves that by removing the physical effects of violence, the violence was stripped of its harm. They showed no blood, no close-ups of agony, no open wounds, no last convulsions of a riddled body. Men were shot, they clapped their hands to their stomachs and either fell forwards or backwards as the camera panned away and returned to the gun. And while the broadcasters felt this a noble concession to the sensibilities of young viewers ("Brutality or physical agony," says the NBC Code, "is not presented in detail nor indicated by offensive sound or visual effects"), they were in actuality presenting, day after day, two great immoralities: that shooting is clean—and easy. To pull a trigger requires neither strength nor skill nor courage: it is the bullet that kills. And to kill with a gun is quick and painless. Hero or criminal, both were cowards who answered questions by pulling triggers. This was the daily lesson for sixty million children for twenty years.

Until, of course, the people finally rose. Some cool legal heads first managed to draft legislation banning the sale of pornographic and sensational printed material without in any way curbing individual liberty or preventing the sale of *Lady Chatterley's Lover* or Aristophanes. And then came the famous FCC ruling Bylaw A 41-632. In effect, this gave the FCC, by then reorganized into a body of able and dedicated communications experts who functioned in areas of human values as well as in electronics, the power to revoke the license of any broadcaster showing fictionalized killing, whether by gun or knife or bludgeon, without also displaying the natural consequences to the person killed. The bill as originally drawn was a forthright ban on all fictionalized killing except by direct bodily means, without weapons: killing had to involve strength, skill, and direct physical involvement. But after long wrangling, the later version was adopted as being less tainted by censorship and more practicable. For if a program showing a killing had to show a head blown to bits at close range, or blood gushing from mouth and nose, or a jagged stomach wound—all natural results of shooting—the sponsor would not sell many goods. It was therefore far easier to cut out guns entirely.

The Violent Society

Far easier, that is, for everyone but the writers. After the law was put into effect, there was mass unemployment among the television writers in Hollywood and New York. They had relied so long on their collaborator, the gun, that they were incapable of writing a plot without it. As Wertham quoted an experienced TV crime writer: "You have to work backwards. You're given a violent situation and you have to work within that framework." Start with the murder and then fit in the people. And suddenly the poor writers had to think up situations where people and ideas provided the excitement instead of a Colt 45. It was a period of anguish none of them will forget.

But for every ten writers who became alcoholics or joined insurance firms, one began to tap resources he had never used and to write well and truly for the first time. And after a hiatus of incredible sterility, when frantic producers threw in anything innocuous, however old and poor, to fill up the time formerly used by crime plays and Westerns, television slowly began to get better and better, more inventive both in the uses of realism and fantasy.

A new generation of American children grew up with no appetite for guns and no illusions about the fun of painless killing. Instead they learned judo or, through compulsory strenuous exercises then conducted daily by their schools, became a race of confident acrobats, able to show their prowess in feats of skill, daring, and endurance without knifing, stomping, or shooting anyone.

Disarmament—at least of the young—was finally a fact.

THE "NIGHT OF HORROR" IN BROOKLYN

SOME YEARS AGO a trial took place in Brooklyn. There was another trial going on at the same time in Cleveland, and that one was big news. It seemed to matter much more whether an osteopath had murdered his pregnant wife than whether four teen-agers had, without reason, beaten and tortured a man until he staggered into the East River and drowned.

Yet it mattered when people first read of it: "Four Brooklyn youths were charged yesterday with a series of crimes that included beating and kicking a man to death, horsewhipping young women and burning the soles of a vagrant's feet, beating him, and throwing him into the river. . . .

" 'I can't understand what would make boys do such terrible things,' Edward S. Silver, Kings County District Attorney, said after hearing their confessions. 'They apparently had no reason except the thrill they got,' he added."—*The New York Times*.

People read excerpts from some of the alleged confessions made by the boys to detectives. "Last night," Koslow was reported as saying when he told of the Negro's drowning, "was the supreme adventure for me. . . . Park bums are no use to society and are better off dead." Mittman, the second boy, was quoted as saying that he used the victims as punching bags "to see how hard I could punch."

For a few days then, horrors hung in the air, and good citizens shook their heads. The boys were put in prison until their trial, and the talk about them subsided. It was too hideous to be sustained, too close for comfort.

For those who saw the trial the horror revived. For here were the boys themselves, ten feet away; not headlines, not files, not cases, but young living beings who had caused death; and for hour after hour one was impelled to examine their features with the same passionate, inquiring intensity with which one listened to the evidence of one terrible night in August.

¶ It was no effort to see evil in Jack Koslow, the oldest defendant. So manifest was his sickness of soul that he could have posed as one of the tormenting demons that populate Hieronymus Bosch's visions of hell. His skin had been described as "sallow," but that gave no hint of its dead green-whiteness, in eerie and surprising conjunction with thick hair that was dark red and wholly without shine, receding from his forehead in a high crest. His features were delicately ugly: a long thin curved nose with a sharply articulated ridge; a thin, downturned, and usually derisive mouth, lips colorless, the upper extending slightly above the lower; a weak but bony chin; a white, undeveloped neck. His eyes were strangest of all. They were dark brown and seemed pupilless, and their look was hooded as if by a transparent extra lid. When Koslow walked in and out each day manacled to his guard, you could see how tall and thin he was, and how his narrow head hung forward from his body like a condor's.

¶ Melvin Mittman, seventeen, was physically his antithesis. His body was barrel-thick and strong, his shoulders wide, his head square, his features blunt. He had an upturned, broad-based nose, small thick-lashed eyes under glasses, dense hair growing low on his brow, and a strong round chin. Throughout the trial until the verdict, when he wept and buried his face in his hands, he was expressionless. You would not have picked him out of a group, as you would Koslow, as having something "wrong" with him; he seemed just stolid and enclosed. Yet where Koslow's hands were white and thin and smooth as a girl's, lacing and interlacing during the trial and drumming little dances, Mittman's hands, abnormally short and thick, with hair on the fingers, made one inevitably imagine them pounding flesh.

¶ The third boy, Jerome Lieberman, also seventeen, was another matter. Here was a diffident, tremulous kid with blinking eyes, a soft mouth, a defenseless neck; the only one of the three defendants to look miserable. Indeed, he was a defendant for only half the trial. He was dismissed for lack of evidence of any direct involvement in this particular case.

¶ The fourth and youngest boy, Robert Trachtenberg, fifteen at the time of the crime, was separated from this trial and appeared only as state's evidence. Tall, darkly handsome, of aristocratic bearing, his speech distinct and mannerly, Trachtenberg inspired one chiefly with incredulity as to the innate viciousness attributed to him—if not in connection with this particular crime, then in involvement in other crimes. As one woman reporter said, "He looks like the kind of boy any mother would be proud of." He looked, more than any of the other three, like the kind of boy who could be salvaged.

Here were the four, then, and this is the story of what they did on the night of August 16, 1954 pieced together by their own words, clinched by an absent but tangible exhibit: the body of Willard Menter dredged from the East River on August 19 and identified by them as the victim of their acts.

The four boys had met by prearrangement this warm summer night. First Trachtenberg picked up Lieberman, his special friend, at the latter's home around eight; then the two met Koslow at the Marcy Avenue subway station; then the three picked up Mittman at his home and off they went.

They discussed what to do. Mittman suggested going to New York and picking up girls. Koslow said no, let's go bum-hunting. It is pertinent to note that in none of the testimony did any of the other three ask what bum-hunting was or argue against it.

The four wandered about rather aimlessly for quite a while until they converged on a place called Triangular Park. "Park" is a euphemism: The triangle is a patch of dusty grass and concrete bordered on three sides by benches and a railing; an island cut off, as it were, from casual access by three intersecting flows of traffic.

The boys stood at the gate of the park. It was about nine o'clock. On a bench at the near side of the triangle two men were sitting, playing chess. On a bench at the far side a man was sleeping, a Negro.

(*"How would you categorize this method," Koslow was asked by Detective Duggan after his arrest, "in which you went out looking for bums?"*

A. *"Just hit or miss. I'd find one. If he was particularly distasteful to either myself or the other boys, the person who he affected most would do what he pleased with him. . . . Sometimes I see a drunken bum, very soused. He looks at you out of one eye. It's disgusting. It incites me to hit him."*)

In Triangular Park the four boys walked over to the sleeping Negro and formed a screen. Koslow was facing his feet, which were bare.

Koslow struck a match and approached a flame to the man's soles, but he did not wake up. Then Koslow lit a cigarette and touched that to the bare brown feet.

(*"What made you use a lit cigarette on this Negro's feet before you took him down to that pier?"*

A. *"Big gag."*)

At the trial, then, Assistant D.A. DeMeo asked Trachtenberg what the Negro did or said. Trachtenberg said that he raised himself half up from the bench, suddenly. "What did he say then?" Trachtenberg, the quiet, subdued, handsome boy, then let out a scream that splintered the courtroom air and was followed by shuddering silence.

So the Negro screamed, he said, and Koslow urged the boys to hit him. The two youngest, he said, himself and Lieberman, demurred. Whether Mittman beat Menter then is not clear. What is clear is that Koslow told the Negro: "Put on your shoes and get up and come with us." And the Negro, scared of this menacing wall of youths and the tone of Koslow's command, put on his shoes and stood up. Koslow and Mittman then flanked him and the three proceeded toward the river, the Negro weaving and staggering, the boys steadying and propelling him on their five-block walk to the pier in the shadow of Williamsburg Bridge.

The two younger boys had asked the older ones at the park where they were going, and when they were told it was the waterfront (*"So we could bang him around in private"*) they hung back, apprehensive. According to Trachtenberg, they split up then for a while until curiosity got the better of them and they went to the pier.

Koslow had told what happened on that soft night, with the water slapping under the barges and at the sides of the rotting pier.

"He [Mittman] hit him with either a right or a left. . . . The bum put his arm up to his face, doubled over and laid sideways over the board that separated the pier from the water. I bent over to punch him. I brought that punch up from the floor. As I was about to land the punch he was in the water, either he slipped or fell. By that I mean he was ducking the punch . . . just as he hit the water; he put his hands forward like this. He didn't just crash into it. Then I saw him in midstream."

"I saw him come up twice and go down again," said Mittman.

Trachtenberg and Lieberman were then standing at a barricade about fifty or a hundred feet back of the pier. (*"They did not have the hatred we did,"* said Koslow.) *Then Trachtenberg heard Mittman's voice calling "Hey, Bob! Come over here!" and then again, "Hey, Bob, you know what Koslow did? He pushed a man in the water!"*

Then, according to Trachtenberg, Koslow came up again and said, "Man's in the water, boys." And young Lieberman said, "Why did you do it?" and then Koslow said, "Now we're all murderers!" and told them to keep quiet. Otherwise, he said, I will get the chair, you [Mittman] will get life, and you two [Trachtenberg and Lieberman] will get five years apiece.

After this they were very quiet and stopped talking about it as they walked home, the younger ones separating from the other two and getting home shortly before midnight. "The river," . . . said Lieberman, "I couldn't sleep all night."

At about five that morning the police came to both. Koslow, arraigned on charges of beating up Kostyra earlier that night, had told of this later event. Mittman was picked up with Koslow.

The parents sat in the courtroom and listened to this day after day, although not all of them every day. On two different occasions Mr. Mittman and Mrs. Koslow collapsed and were taken away. But usually Mr. and Mrs. Koslow sat together, apart from the other parents, and Mrs. Mittman sat next to Mr. and Mrs. Lieberman.

Mrs. Koslow was small with bleached hair. Her face was tight and rather empty, and she wore glasses. She bore no resemblance to her son. But Koslow's father's face was the aging matrix of his son's: the same shape of head and bones, but crushed and sagging with grief.

Mr. and Mrs. Mittman might have been the couple who ran the cleaning shop or the stationer's next door. They were short, well dressed, self-respecting in manner. They seemed like good people, and such was their reputation. The mother had given the son her features, but while they were pleasing in her they were only coarse and immature in him. Mrs. Mittman's face was controlled in court, but blurred by nightly tears.

Mr. and Mrs. Lieberman, too, looked like good people, quiet and middle-class. Mrs. Lieberman was a strong woman, broad-boned and east European in feature, while her husband, bald and myopic, seemed mild and complaisant.

Again and again at the trial one looked at these parents and asked—as they asked themselves—what had they done to produce such issue as these? What had they failed to do?

Koslow's attorney, State Senator Fred G. Moritt, was unusual in his role of lawyer and seeker after justice. Dressed like a song writer (he was a successful one and a member of A.S.C.A.P.), theatrical in his many objections and interpolations, he seemed a little out of place in a court otherwise imbued by Judge Hyman Barshay's uncompromising dignity.

Basing his defense of Koslow on "mischief," Moritt struck an odd note as he wound up his summation by reading to the jury a verse of his own contriving (based on "Ten Little Indians"):

> Four little bad boys off on a spree,
> One turned state's evidence, and then there were three.
> Three little bad boys, what did one do?
> The Judge said, "No proof" and then there were two.
> Two little bad boys, in court they must sit
> And pray to the Jury, "Please, please acquit."

No one in the courtroom smiled except Moritt and Koslow.

Before this, Moritt had deplored the death of Menter, vagrant though he was, by intoning the words of another poet, John Donne: "Any man's death diminishes me. . . ."

It was implied during the trial that the death of Willard Menter did not diminish society. Menter ran a blower in a secondhand burlap-bag factory, surely a lowly pursuit; and his only happiness seemed to consist in occasional binges that he would sleep off on park benches. The best that was said of him was spoken by his brother: "Willie, he'd drink a little bit, but he didn't start no fights." His life was without much sense and his death was without any sense. But it was precisely the senselessness of his death that made this crime both terrible and important, throwing into blinding focus the one great question not only of the trial but of the time: Why Did They Do It?

It was the law's concern to establish whether they did it and how they did it, not why. And when it had been shown to the jury's satisfaction that Jack Koslow and Melvin Mittman had caused the death of Willard Menter, the law had done its part. At the end of the trial nothing was known of these boys because nothing was asked.

Outside the courtroom, though, one man in particular did ask questions. He was Dr. Fredric Wertham, who was senior

The Violent Society

psychiatrist for the Department of Hospitals in New York City from 1932 to 1952, directing the mental-hygiene clinics at Bellevue Hospital and Queens Hospital Center. Dr. Wertham, who has published two books on juvenile delinquency, *The Show of Violence* and *Seduction of the Innocent* (the influence of comic books on today's youth), was called in by the court to determine whether Jack Koslow could plead legal insanity. After examination of Koslow, Wertham's findings on this point were negative: The boy knew what he had done and was aware of right and wrong—for others, at least. Neither the court nor Koslow's counsel, Moritt, went further. Legal insanity was out, and that was that.

But Wertham went further. He got permission from Judge Barshay to examine Koslow as much as he wished before the trial, and the psychiatrist spent many hours with the boy, gaining his confidence. Since he believed that the violation of this confidence was not only permissible in such special circumstances, but might be helpful in the interests of truth, Wertham told this writer the essence of these interviews. What follows is a paraphrase of Wertham's notes and comments on Koslow.

Koslow is a very intelligent boy: well read, well spoken, with a glibness that is enormously persuasive. ("His intelligence is like a knife without a handle. . . .") By his own admission, he has been able to talk anybody into anything.

He is the only son of a middle-class family intent, as most Americans are, on improving their place in the world. The Koslows lived first on the lower East Side of Manhattan, then moved to the Williamsburg section of Brooklyn, and finally to Flatbush, where Koslow's father is an industrious and skilled auto mechanic. Their son has never suffered privation, but he claims that he has always hated his father and oriented himself toward his doting mother.

The first overt sign of this abnormality came at seven, when Koslow was referred to the Bureau of Child Guidance as being too difficult to handle, both at school and at home. Dr. Harry

But Will It Sell?

Gilbert, the supervisor of psychiatrists for this board, said that he was found to be "aggressive and subject to fantasies about killings." He had also a vociferous love of the Nazis, expressed partly by crying "Heil Hitler!" in class. This was in 1942, when the Nazis were at their crest; and Koslow told Wertham that his love of fascism and force, of irresistible brutality, of a supreme "elite," started then.

He was examined by Dr. Abram Blau, among others, at the Bureau. Dr. Blau, a psychiatrist of the highest reputation, reported that the child had been disturbed from early childhood and strongly recommended treatment.

According to Gilbert, Koslow was given four treatments, and his parents were interviewed by the Bureau. But then Mrs. Koslow became ill and took the boy out of school for a month, and when he returned the treatments were discontinued.

Koslow remembered Blau well. He told Wertham he wished his father had been like Blau.

The boy was physically very under par: He had all the childhood diseases and at nine trouble with his legs—a systemic swelling and weakness that, he says, handicapped and depressed him.

In all his contacts, at school or at home, Koslow was argumentative, domineering, discontented. He could get on with others only if he could influence them; and as he found it difficult to influence his teachers, he was constantly at loggerheads with them in spite of his high I.Q. (at nine, 135) and his genuine scholastic abilities. Because of these he was put in a class for "gifted children" in high school, but instead of being gratified by this distinction, he resented keenly what he referred to as being "put apart"—isolated even more from his fellows.

Koslow got through high school in three years, graduating at sixteen. During this time he had also managed to teach himself German, the language of his idols.

In 1952 he went to New York University to take a dental course at the urging of his mother, but he was so obviously intractable that the university authorities sent him to the Testing and Advisement Center, one of the best clinics in the country, for psychiatric examination. There another eminent man, Dr. Wallace Gobetz, reported that Koslow was either psychotic or on the verge of psychosis, and sent him to Dr. J. Allison Montagu, who made a diagnosis of "incipient schizophrenia," recommending intensive treatment.

The youth's parents, dismayed and angry that their son was virtually suspended from the university because of his alleged condition, took him instead to a private psychiatrist who signed a report testifying that there was nothing wrong with Koslow and that he should be accepted at N.Y.U. for further courses. In February, 1953, the youth spent another very brief period at the university and got along so badly that he left of his own accord. "I was a failure," he said.

Subsequently he went to work, holding about six different jobs for brief periods. There was always something wrong with the job, he said. He found fault with everything and everyone. And from June, 1954, onward, Koslow was one of the unemployed, sleeping much of the day, roaming much of the night, hunting for bums.

"I'm a fascist," Koslow told Wertham simply. "I always have been. I'm a fascist and a white supremacist. Everybody is, really. That's all the talk you hear around anyway. . . . Violence? It's everywhere. All I'm interested in is violence—destruction—death." These were his actual words.

He told Wertham (whose identity he was not told) that he was an addict of horror comics. "There's some guy," he said, "a psychiatrist—who keeps saying they have a bad effect on kids. I read about it in the *Reader's Digest*. Listen—I could tell that guy something!"

Wertham told Koslow he was "that guy" and the boy seemed amused. On one of his visits Wertham brought him a paper-covered set of "Nights of Horror," in fourteen thin volumes. "Is this the sort of thing you read?" he asked. Koslow leafed through them and nodded. "That's it. Only I have a better edition."

But Will It Sell?

For the benefit of those who had not seen the publications, they constituted what Wertham called "the pornography of violence." The illustrations were chiefly concerned with voluptuous women in a minimum of suggestive underwear being tortured in a variety of ways: bull-whipped, burned with cigarettes, strangled with wire, and so forth. They in turn inflicted certain elaborate punishments on men, of a clearly sexual nature. The text was cigar-store Spillane, more explicit in its sadism, more viciously saccharine in its "romantic" passages.

"Nights of Horror" might leave the mature adult with no other reaction but disgust. What it might do to the immature—even the "normal" immature—is anybody's guess. In any case, it was likely that Koslow and his companions had tried many of the refinements in the series. He even told Wertham that they had made one of their beating victims kiss their feet in between blows and kicks, a scene clearly illustrated in "Nights of Horror." "It is hardly something," said Wertham, "that a boy would do spontaneously—that is, without getting the idea from somewhere."

"Nights of Horror" had been banned, but thousands of copies were then still circulating, under counters and in private collections.

Koslow had in his room a collection of bull whips. One of them, for which he paid $3.75, he ordered through an advertisement in a comic book, either "Uncanny Tales" or "Journey into Mystery." He also carried a switch-blade knife which he got from a schoolmate who bought it through a comic book. Under the new comic-book code, such advertisements are banned, although this does not mean that the supply houses no longer exist.

Koslow owned a "costume" consisting of black pants, black boots, black shirt, black jacket, and black gloves in which he acted his role of "vampire" at night. Sometimes he wore them all; on the night of the Menter killing, he wore the black pants. The vampire suit is an old standby in horror comics, merely a more sinister version of the tight over-all ritualistic uniform of the superman, good or evil.

The Violent Society

In Koslow's statement to Detective Duggan when he was taken to the pier to identify Menter's body, he said (of the moment after Menter was in the water): *"I just saw the belly float—float."* (In a comic book, a thug who has just watched a victim drown says, "Makes a pretty bubble, doesn't it?")

Koslow and Mittman were ostensibly a loyal and devoted pair. When they heard the jury's verdict of first-degree murder with recommendation of life imprisonment, and Koslow groaned and Mittman wept, Koslow put his arm around the other boy. The two seemed to function as mind and body, Koslow doing the planning and direction, Mittman—usually shy and quiet—the rough stuff. Koslow himself did virtually none of the fighting.

"He likes crime comics," said Koslow with amused contempt of his partner. "You know, 'Superman' and all that." Crime-comic addiction was clearly of a lower order than horror addiction: kid stuff.

Although several psychiatrists who had never seen the boys announced respectively at the time of their arrests that they were either rapists or homosexuals or both, Wertham found no evidence to support either claim. He said Koslow was sexually underdeveloped and misdeveloped, that none of the boys were really concerned with sex even when they talked of girls. What bound the four together was a compulsion to watch other people in agony.

They also needed to assert superiority, to "Be Somebody." Mittman said he punched bums because it made him "feel big and strong." Koslow said, "I had to do it to preserve my individuality."

According to Wertham, Koslow was primarily a masochist, both perpetrator and victim in an equation too complex for discussion here. Yet Wertham believes he could have been "saved" and his energies and talents channeled into constructive outlets had he availed himself of the advice and treatment offered him from the age of six onward. He might never have been a "success" or a whole man or an attractive human being. But he need never have been a threat to society, Wertham thinks.

The other three boys—Mittman, Lieberman, and Trachtenberg—appear to have no psychiatric history at all. Yet no one knows how many girls they may have horsewhipped or how many "bums" they may have kicked and beaten.

In the files of the police department and in the memories of seasoned police officers, crimes such as theirs were virtually unknown before the Second World War. Exceptions like the Leopold and Loeb case only proved the rule. Boys under eighteen may have killed out of sudden rage or performed acts of violence, but boys under eighteen from "good homes" did not torture and kill for pleasure. This was something new. And it is something that exists on a greater scale than we dream of: The partners Youth and Brutality have pushed the delinquency rate in this country to an all-time high.

No informed and responsible person will say that the roots of this epidemic of violence are horror comics or crime comics or gangster movies or crime plays on television or the crime-laden tabloids. But a number of informed and responsible people say that their cumulative effect on young minds may be an important factor. Certainly a hundred boys could read "Nights of Horror" or "Uncanny Tales" and commit no acts of violence. But who is there to say that the hundred and first, as sick as Koslow, as weak as Lieberman, might not? If there is indeed a virus of violence abroad (and the evidence is enormous), then should it not be located and controlled like any disease, for the protection of the susceptible—and of society itself?

The police will tell you that to many delinquents nowhere nearly as sick as Koslow, violence is the natural order of things. "It's all around . . . ."

It is not up to the courts to solve the why of this particular Brooklyn murder or of others destined to be committed by the young. It is up to society.

We must find ways to prevent the stupidity or ignorance or fear of parents who, seeing the danger signals flown, do not heed them.

We must find the causes of this susceptibility in the young, this vacuum that can be filled with violence, this boredom than can be relieved by the suffering of others. What is it that they miss and do not have? Why is action equated with destruction, adventure with death?

Koslow and Mittman, they say, went to the Synagogue. Trachtenberg and Lieberman liked books and music. But where did ethics come in, or a simple regard for life?

We must find out if the backwash of the last great war has left this wrack; whether killing for cause is a prelude to or preparation for killing without cause.

These are some of the questions we must ask ourselves, so that before there is much more time for this horror, we can act on the answers.

NOTE: In early 1955 Trachtenberg was committed to Cedar Knolls, a New York youth institute, and Koslow and Mittman got life sentences with no possibility of parole except by executive pardon.

Three years later a new trial was ordered by the New York State Appellate Division for Koslow and Mittman in which they pleaded not guilty. Later, they reversed their plea to guilty and got 10-20 years for 1st Degree Manslaughter.

THE MURDER OF IN HO OH

THE CRIME was appalling because it was wholly without motive. It might have happened to anyone who crossed Hamilton Avenue at Thirty-sixth Street in

But Will It Sell?

Philadelphia at nine o'clock on the evening of April 25, 1958. There is nothing particularly sinister about the street or the neighborhood. Heavy-leaved trees line the sidewalk and half obscure the wood-and-stucco houses with their porches and pillars, slightly melancholy for lack of paint and an air of past gentility. Most are now filled with roomers: students from the University of Pennsylvania, ten blocks or so away, and white and colored people of modest means.

A Korean student named In Ho Oh lived with his aunt and uncle in a small and bare apartment in a corner house. His purpose in leaving that night was to mail a letter in the mailbox diagonally across the street. His misfortune was to be on the street when eleven teen-age Negroes came by after having been turned away from a neighborhood dance—some, it seems, because of "improper attire" and some for lack of the admission price of sixty-five cents. According to newspaper reports the following day, they met other youths and told them what had happened. "At that point," a Juvenile Aid officer said, "these kids were ready to fight and probably would have attacked the first person they met on the street."

At least eight of the boys involved set upon the small, slight Korean student and beat him to death with a lead pipe, fists, shoes, and a blackjack. When he was a bloody pulp on the sidewalk, one of them is said to have shouted, "I've got his wallet. There's no money in it." Then they all ran away. In Ho Oh died ten minutes later.

For years men like Director Maurice Fagan of the Fellowship Commission in Philadelphia and many others in Jewish, Quaker, Protestant, and Catholic groups in Philadelphia have been trying —with some success—to educate their people in three concepts: that the answer to the brutality of crime is not brutality of law, for violence merely begets violence; that delinquency is bred not of race but of acute economic and social depression that disintegrates the family unit; and that if the incidence of Negro crime is high in the city, the deprivations of the Negro community and the indifference of their established neighbors has much to do with it. Of the half million Negroes in Philadelphia, the majority live in squalor.

"After this," Fagan said, "we have been set back ten years. The attitudes have hardened: black against white, white against black. Compassion has been replaced by fear. And you cannot blame people," he said reluctantly, "for being afraid."

The murder of In Ho Oh was indeed enough to cause shock and abhorrence as well as fear. And though the nature of the victim of a murder should not be a measure of the nature of the act, in this case the qualities of the young Korean brought the horror of the crime and its perpetrators into sharper focus.

His Uncle Ki Hang Oh and his young Aunt Za Young Oh remember every moment of the day he was killed and the night after it and the many nightmares of the next few weeks. Ki Hang, a stocky man of thirty-seven, was working for a doctorate in Assyriology at Dropsie College and had a full-time job besides to support himself, Za Young, and their two children, who live with their grandparents in Korea. His young wife had arrived only five months before from Pusan to join her husband and study singing at the University of Pennsylvania. She spoke little English, but she often corrected or amplified her husband's account in soft Korean, which he then translated for my benefit.

"He was so happy that day," said Ki Hang. "I remember him that morning, so neatly dressed—he never wore sport clothes, always very formal and neat, with his hair oiled and his shoes polished, and his clean white shirt and tie.

"I think that he was happy because at last he did not have to work so hard at night. He was always tired before; you know it is tiring to study all day and work all night. My nephew, first he ran an elevator in a bank, and then lately they gave him other work, lighter work, and he had more time to study. Also he was happy because he liked his studies in political science more than at first. You know, he wished to be a statesman in Korea, and we all knew he would be a wonderful statesman. He wanted so much to help his people."

In Ho, I learned, had been first in his class at high school in

But Will It Sell?

Seoul and one of the top three at the Seoul National University. He came to the United States as an exchange student on a scholarship and was graduated in philosophy from Eastern Baptist College in 1957.

"Perhaps," said his uncle, "when I speak of my nephew I make him too beautiful," and then, correcting himself, "too nice." But all who knew In Ho said the same things of him: that he was brilliant, shy, kind, perceptive, and full of great promise. He was, as all his family were and are, a practicing and dedicated Christian. He had a clear vision of what he wanted to be and do, and both images merged with the future of his people.

"My nephew," said Ki Hang, "did not believe in violence, he did not understand violence. If somebody would hit him, he would not think of defending himself." He did not add that In Ho had neither time nor chance on that night in April, even if the thought of defense had occurred.

The uncle then spoke of that night. He and his wife were resting on their beds, exhausted after the day's work. They heard In Ho leave his room and go out, and thought he was leaving for his job at the Provident Tradesmens Bank. Some time later they heard a knock on the door and Mrs. Oh went to answer it. It was dark and a man was outside and asked, "Does a Chinese or a Korean live with you here?" Then there were other people and police cars and policemen and lights, and Mrs. Oh became more and more confused and fearful and went to rouse her husband. When he came to the door, a policeman showed him a ball-point pen and asked, "Does this belong to your nephew?" Ki Hang said "Yes"; In Ho had just bought several like it. And then they told him what had happened.

"I lay on my bed then and could not rise. I could do nothing. I was overwhelmed. I could not move." So the uncle and aunt lay in a trance of horror while their friend, fellow student, and neighbor, Y. C. Kim, spoke for them to the police and then went with them to identify what was left of In Ho.

The Ohs were a prominent family in North Korea, where they

128

The Violent Society

had lived for generations before they fled from the Russians to the south after the Second World War: a large, affluent, and public-spirited clan who managed miraculously to preserve their family unity—in spirit at least—through half a century of Japanese occupation, Communist harassment, flight, dislocation, the Korean War, and all the successive dangers, deprivations, and deaths these events had brought upon them. Ki Hang himself went to high school in Manchuria, to a university in Japan, then back to South Korea during the war, where he was taken prisoner by the North Koreans and held for several months.

"I have seen many horrible things in these years," he said, "but not anything so horrible as what occurred to my nephew, for it had no meaning. I know of the Japanese atrocities and I know they were horrible. But they were not without reason: the Japanese did this for their country and their Emperor. The boys who killed my nephew had no reason." Yet when Ki Hang mentioned the Negro boys he did so with a strange detachment. Not once did he use the word "murder," and the phrase "when my nephew died" came most often to his lips.

The shock waves that hit Philadelphia were felt thousands of miles away. Although Ki Hang Oh had immediately sent a cable to In Ho's parents in Seoul telling them of the tragedy, it reached them only after they had read of it in the Korean papers. They telephoned him: "Can this possibly be true?"

By this time, the conscience of Philadelphia made itself felt. The press and Mayor Richardson Dilworth gave full expression to the surge of shame and horror. Because In Ho had been a civilian interpreter with the U.S. Army during the Korean War, two women volunteers in the local Red Cross chapter undertook to provide communication between the family in Korea and the family in Philadelphia, and they assisted in the painful and complex processes of In Ho's funeral and the disposition of his body. At first the Hos felt that it should be returned to Korea so that the ancient rituals involving his parents' presence at the internment could be consummated. A maze of obstacles, including prolonged delay in transporting the casket, made this impossible, and it was decided in family council to cremate his remains and ship his ashes for burial there. But this decision in turn was rescinded by In Ho's parents. This letter made their reasons clear:

PUSAN, KOREA

DIRECTOR
PHILADELPHIA RED CROSS

DEAR SIR:

We, the parents of In Ho Oh, on behalf of our whole family, deeply appreciate the expressions of sympathy you have extended to us at this time. In Ho had almost finished the preparation needed for the achievement of his ambition, which was to serve his people and nation as a Christian statesman. His death by an unexpected accident leaves that ambition unachieved.

When we heard of his death, we could not believe the news was true, for the shock was so unexpected and sad, but now we find that it is an undeniable fact that In Ho has been killed by a gang of Negro boys whose souls were not saved and in whom human nature is paralyzed. We are sad now, not only because of In Ho's unachieved future, but also because of the unsaved souls and paralyzed human nature of the murderers.

We thank God that He has given us a plan whereby our sorrow is being turned into Christian purpose. It is our hope that we may somehow be instrumental in the salvation of the souls, and in giving life to the human nature of the murderers. Our family has met together and we have decided to petition that the most generous treatment possible within the laws of your government be given to those who have committed this criminal action without knowing what it would mean to him who has been sacrificed, to his family, to his friends, and to his country.

In order to give evidence of our sincere hope contained in this petition, our whole family has decided to save money to start a fund to be used for the religious, educational, vocational, and social guidance of the boys when they are released. In addition, we are daring to hope that we can do something to minimize such juvenile criminal actions which are to be found, not only in your country, but also in Korea, and, we are sure, everywhere in the world.

About the burial of the physical body of him who has been sacrificed; we hope that you could spare a piece of land in your country and bury it there, for your land, too, is homeland for Christians and people of the democratic society, and it is our sincere hope that thus we will remember your people, and you will remember our people, and that both you and we will more vitally sense an obligation for the better guidance of juvenile delinquents whose souls are unsaved, and whose human natures are paralyzed. We hope in this way to make his tomb a monument which will call attention of people to this cause. We think this is a way to give life to the dead, and to the murderers, and to keep you and us closer in Christian love and fellowship.

We are not familiar with your customs and you may find something hard to understand in what we are trying to say and do. Please interpret our hope and idea with Christian spirit and in the light of democratic principles. We have dared to express our hope with a spirit received from the Gospel of our Savior Jesus Christ who died for our sins.

May God bless you, your people, and particularly the boys who killed our son and kinsman.

> KI BYANG OH (father)
> President, Yung-Chin Industrial Company
> SHIN WYNN H. OH (mother)

The letter was signed also by two uncles, two aunts, five sisters, two brothers, and nine cousins.

The funeral services were held in a small chapel in West Philadelphia. To represent his parents, In Ho's older uncle, Ki Song Oh, who was completing his master of arts degree in international law at the university in Austin, Texas, was flown to Philadelphia so that he could attend the ceremony—with the aid and resources, once more, of the Red Cross chapter. There were about fifty mourners—Korean fellow students of In Ho, his professors, close friends, and community leaders. A large number of Negroes lived in the neighborhood, but no Negroes were to be seen. Fearfully and silently they peered through their windows at the coffin and the mourners.

Mayor Dilworth spoke and wept. The handsome, war-toughened ex-Marine said in a broken voice, "It is a horrible thing that this could happen in our city." At the close of the service he stood apart from the others, looking down at the sealed casket.

The young Korean finally came to rest in the consecrated ground of the Old Pine Street Presbyterian Church in the company of Philadelphia's honored Americans.

But Will It Sell?

Though their nephew's body was in peace and the boys who killed him had been arraigned and the good people of the city were offering help and kindness at every turn, Ki Hang Oh and his wife could no longer bear to remain in the street where In Ho Oh had died. They kept seeing his face and hearing his voice. And there were mysterious telephoned threats, the psychotic wake of crime and horror. Police were stationed to protect the Ohs and follow them everywhere, but still they felt they had to move away.

After a fruitless search for a shelter within their means, a director of the Red Cross chapter offered to take them into his home. "Even here," he said, "on the top floor, with my family all around them and police outside, they were filled with fear. I could hear Mrs. Oh pacing the floor of her room at four in the morning, night after night."

"We are very careful now—very careful," said Ki Hang Oh.

And what of the cause of their terror and their loss, the boys who had killed? The police had rounded most of them up within a few hours of the crime. "Our Gang Control Squad," said the inspector in charge of the Juvenile Aid Bureau, "knows all the gangs in each neighborhood and we had plenty of clues." In the course of time these facts came to light:

Their ages ranged from fifteen to nineteen, and they came from the lowest income group in the city, from broken homes and slum neighborhoods. Several of them had records of previous arrests. Two bore proud American names: Douglas Mac-Arthur Clark and Franklin Marshall. One, the eldest, was retarded. And in refutation of a popular theory that newcomers from the South are the root of the trouble, all the boys were Philadelphia-born, though their parents may have come from the South. In speaking of this migration, Director of Parole Dr. John Otto Rememann suggested that boys of this age, black or white, suffered particularly from parental neglect, for their mothers had entered defense plants during the war, leaving them to a life on the streets without guidance, home, or family. "These boys were born, you see, in the 1940's."

The Violent Society

Philadelphia felt an almost personal shame for them: an emotion apparently alien to New York, which is too big, too complex, and too diffuse to feel responsibility for the crimes committed daily on its streets. It may also be that Philadelphia's conscience has been prodded chiefly by the traditions of its Quaker and Jewish groups. For although the city has bred individuals of great distinction and service of other faiths and affiliations, there is a cohesion among the Friends and the Jews that gives them particular strength.

But for the average citizen, the shame felt for these boys was coupled not so much with a sense of responsibility for their condition as with a loathing that found its quickest release in fear and hysteria. The first stunned reaction to the Christian charity the Ohs had shown changed from incredulity and admiration to a mounting demand for vengeful action. Although the Negro papers, often shrill with their own hysteria of resentment and blame of whites, exaggerated when they wrote of a "pre-trial 'lynch atmosphere,'" the editor of the Philadelphia *Courier* spoke the simple truth when he said: "Most tragic of all regarding civil stability is that when crimes are committed by Negro youths, public indignation turns upon the Negro race, sparing none."

It had also turned, with fury, on all forms of sociological explanation, on all efforts at understanding basic causes, at all corrective measures that are not immediate and merciless. "The public," said Mr. Fagan sadly, "is willing to spend unlimited funds for whipping posts, in spite of the fact that there is conclusive proof that 'the works' don't work any more than 'softness' does." And the inspector of Juvenile Aid himself admitted that strong-arm methods by the police alone were of little avail.

"We did a month's experiment with gangs of delinquents," he said, "harassing them all the time, arresting them, sitting on their necks, throwing them in jail for the smallest offenses, and at the end of that time the incidence of crimes among them only increased. We found that the only way we could get anywhere was through the active co-operation of the community where they lived—with their teachers and their parents, with civic groups and social workers. And for two years now we have had special officers on our force who have been trained in community relations at the University of Pennsylvania.

"It's a slow process, and there are no quick answers. But we seem to have made some progress in one area at least, and that's in the use of weapons. Ever since our judges have clamped down hard on kids for the mere possession of weapons, you don't see so many. They're afraid to get caught with them. The boys in this case mostly used hands and feet—except for pop bottles and that one blackjack."

The public had demanded a quick end to its fears and an assurance of safety through harsh means; the district attorney had promised to exact utmost penalties for this hideous crime. But the wise men, the good men, and the brave men of the town knew better—the mayor himself, the Juvenile Aid inspector, the director of paroles, the head of the new and shining Youth Study Center where the delinquent boys and girls are held before they are brought to trial or returned to their homes.

In a broadcast soon after the murder the mayor spoke on the whole subject of delinquency in Philadelphia. He mentioned the flood of mail he had received urging immediate and repressive action and underlaid with racial animus, and he said, among other things: "I think it is helpful to give a specific example of the terrible harm that is reaped upon a community by inhuman, repressive measures," and he told of the way Negroes lived in Johannesburg and were treated there. "Any Negro found on the street at night is shot on sight. Yet, today, Johannesburg has the highest incidence of Negro crimes of violence of any city in the world, and the white population does not dare venture on the streets at night without armed protection. I just do not think that we can emphasize enough that man's inhumanity to man simply results in increased violence and evil."

In discussing solutions, the mayor said: "The fundamental reason so many juveniles have been released on probation is that our state is unfortunately almost a hundred years behind the times in providing the essential facilities for dealing with juvenile problems. . . . Today we have no facility whatsoever in the state to which mentally disturbed or backward girls can be sent. There is absolutely no facility operated by the state for mentally disturbed or backward boys under sixteen years of age. There is absolutely no state institution where juveniles who are just starting to turn bad and need a good, sharp, short lesson can be sent. . . ." And there was no place at all where those who have served their sentences can be prepared for a return to freedom: a sort of decompression chamber for emergence into normal society.

"I myself," he said later, "have appeared at four successive sessions of the legislature to urge the necessary appropriations for these essential facilities, but have been told that there has been no evidence of any citizen interest; on the contrary, that the citizens are demanding a decrease in so-called welfare expenditures."

And as if to disprove this charge and to answer the flood of questions from a presumably awakened citizenry as to what they themselves could do to stem this tide of youthful crime, the mayor listed twenty-two organizations and activities that an individual could join in the fight against delinquency. The broadcast was estimated to have reached many tens of thousands in the city. Ninety-four Philadelphians volunteered their services.

Although the mayor took pains to make clear that the high rate of crime among Philadelphia's half million Negroes was an inevitable result of the appalling conditions in which many were forced to live and the attendant human disintegrations, he did not absolve the Negro community of its share of guilt.

"There is also a regrettable scarcity of leadership in the Negro communities in the large cities. That is largely due to the fact that only some ninety years have elapsed since the days of slavery and very little opportunity has been open to them in fields which create leadership. . . . I think the one real criticism that can be leveled at some of the important elements of the Negro community is that they demand, as they should, their rights as first-class citizens, but at the same time seek to retain the privileges and special considerations of a distinctly minority group. They must do more to help themselves . . . ."

Mrs. Oh had only this to say of the boys who killed her nephew: "Not one of their families wrote to share our sorrow. In our country people in their position would have done so." She might also have added that no matter how grinding their poverty, Asian mothers do not leave their children on the street but preserve, above all, the family unit. It is an established fact that of all the minorities in this country the Chinese have the lowest crime rate.

"Our main purpose now," said Mr. Fagan of the Fellowship Commission, "is to keep some line of communication open between whites and Negroes, so that they can at least still talk to each other. If that is lost, everything else goes too."

NOTE: Three years after the murder of the young Korean, justice had caught up with the perpetrators to the extent of ten convictions with stiff sentences and two retrials—one involving a death sentence—pending.

In the meantime the Oh family had managed to save $500—a remarkable feat in a country where workers make from 2 to 35 cents a day—to set up a memorial fund which would provide a yearly award to the boy scout troop doing the most to improve conditions in the Powelton district, the neighborhood of the crime.

The conscience of Philadelphia expressed itself in a fund to provide milk for Korean children; in a mobile medical unit for the Korean Health Ministry; in a scholarship fund for Koreans at the University of Pennsylvania that grew to $12,000 and has already afforded two years of graduate study for a nuclear physicist and an electrical engineer; and in a four-year scholarship at Eastern Baptist University, of which the first recipient was a nineteen-year-old girl cousin of In Ho Oh who has since graduated and hopes to teach English in Korea.

And on the headstone of the murdered student's grave in the Old Pine Street Presbyterian cemetery are these words from his parents' letter: To Turn Sorrow into Christian Purpose.

THE LONG VIGIL

THERE ARE MOMENTS of such magnitude that they must be clearly remembered. And it might serve a purpose to record what one American—and surely multitudes more—saw and felt and thought sitting before the television set on a Friday and a Saturday and a Sunday and a Monday in November, 1963.

This was not viewing. This was total involvement.

I was out when the President was shot and saw only the replayed tape, first of him waving and smiling to cheering Dallas faces, mostly young, and then the wild, careening moment of the murder: the insane kaleidoscope in the camera's eye as it swung and jolted from a photographer running through chaos to commotion. From then on, with few intervals away, I stayed before the set, knowing—as millions knew—that I must give myself over entirely to an appalling tragedy, and that to evade it was a treason of the spirit.

It is hard to remember the exact sequence of events that Friday; incredulity and shock at this immense unreason left no place for an orderly succession in the mind. It was all ambulances and police cars and corridors and bewildered newsmen holding up microphones to bewildered people, and once in a while the small figure of the President's wife, briefly recognized and then eclipsed.

The sunny streets of Dallas were cruel and ugly, the warehouse walls with those terrible open windows were cruel and ugly, there was a glaring tawdriness about everything there, from the fat police to the sleek ambulance to the thruway that led to the hospital. What two hours ago was merely a commercial city in broad noon was now a blatant nightmare.

Later there was the scene in the plane when a woman judge swore in the big man with the scored face as President of the United States, and Mrs. Johnson and Mrs. Kennedy stood by; and you tried to take it in, and you tried to find solace in the orderly quiet succession, brief and simple, but you could not: it was too much to take. Through those hours too you saw the face of Lee Oswald, thin and pasty and small-mouthed, and you thought what a miserable worm he was and how even hate for him was overwhelmed by horror of his act. And then when you heard them say he was a Marxist you thought oh God, it is bad enough without this, here we go, from now on the old hysteria has fuel to burn on again. And you thought of the smugness and relief of the rightists and the wise shaking of many heads over leftist subversives, and what this would do to us in the time to come.

In the partly sleepless night that followed, the distorted echoes of an ancient ballad repeated and repeated through my head: "Where are you going, Lee Oswald my son?/ To the post office, Mother, to get me a gun./ For there's hate in my heart and there's hate in my head,/ And I'm going to shoot the President dead."

It was only later, much later, when the plane that carried the President's body and the President's wife and their successors arrived in Andrews Air Force Base, that the implacable sequence began; or seemed to begin.

I sat there watching men struggling through the door of the plane's hydraulic lift with the casket and I thought, there he is, and I thought of that shattered head underneath and the high shoulders and long legs and how he looked when he walked into press conferences with a quick step and his thick-haired head slightly bent forward and his down-slanted eyes slightly quizzical. And I watched Mrs. Kennedy being helped down to the ground by two men and follow the casket to the ambulance and step into it with her brother-in-law, and I wondered what made it possible for a woman so like a girl to look at this long metal box.

The Violent Society

As for us, the millions, we could not take our eyes from the metal box. It was not morbidity, it was a desperate attachment, a holding on to what was already lost until there was not even this rectangle and remnant to cling to. I followed it every inch of the way, I watched each time the nine proud young men bore the heaviest burden of their lives up the steps and into the White House, down the steps and onto the caisson, up the steps to the Capitol, down the steps of the Capitol, back to the White House, into the Cathedral, out of the Cathedral and then, finally, on to the grave. I imagined them telling of this till the day they died; of how they carried the President and what it felt like to know his body was in their hands.

I followed the caisson every step it went down the broad avenues from home to Hill, from Hill to home and from home to earth. The simplicity of that box with the flag on it, the great loneliness of the executive in death as in life, were made just bearable by the sturdy gray horses, nuzzling and jerking against their traces, by the beautiful ridden horse with his high head and rhythmic gait, by the fretting and rearing riderless black horse behind, by the single sailor with the President's flag. I was grateful every inch of the way for these traditions, for the awful solemnity of the muffled drums; I was proud of the silence they beat in and the grief they echoed.

And I, like millions, was immeasurably proud of the President's wife. Nothing will ever erase from my mind the sight of that small erect black figure with the sightless eyes of a caryatid and the features of Greek tragedy standing on the steps of the White House or the steps of the Capitol with her small children holding her hands. Her control, her grace, her dignity were miracles, demanding from us who watched a restraint which we could not always match, since we could contain only a part of her grief.

Hour after hour, wherever the President lay, I watched the people who came to honor him. The familiar faces of senators and judges, of Cabinet members, of the family itself were made less familiar by the shock and strain that ennobled them. Most of them looked years older.

139

But Will It Sell?

Hour after hour I watched the people without names file past the catafalque in the Rotunda, the elders looking at the bier, the children distracted by the lights and guards. And then Mrs. Kennedy came with Caroline tightly holding her hand and John fidgeting as she looked before her. I saw Caroline flapping her free white-gloved hand and I wondered what was growing in her mind, and I saw John taken away, and I watched Mrs. Kennedy and Caroline, now still and grave, kneel at the bier while Mrs. Kennedy kissed the flag on it. Every movement she made was right; and hard to bear.

And during all this—the shuffle of the feet, the tolling of bells, the beating of drums, the clopping of horses' hooves, the click of the honor guard's rifles, the shrilling of whistles—during all of this, for four interminable days, I listened to the familiar voices of those men whom we are highly privileged as a people to have as interpreters of events: Edward P. Morgan and Howard K. Smith, Walter Cronkite and Eric Sevareid and Charles Collingwood, Chet Huntley and David Brinkley, Marvin Kalb and Robert Pierpoint, and so many more who never failed us or history during their greatest possible ordeal. Shaken as they visibly were, infinitely weary as they became, they maintained calm and reason and insight throughout the marathon of madness and mourning.

The madness punctuated the mourning, as millions watched, that Sunday afternoon in Dallas. I could not believe what I saw. The clutter of newsmen and their microphones in that basement corridor, the milling and talking, and then those big fat men bringing the thin pasty prisoner, and then the back of a man with a hat, and then Oswald doubled, and then pandemonium, scuffles, shouts and young Tom Truitt and his microphone in and out of the picture trying to find out what happened. Questions seethed through my mind: how in God's name could the police expose a President's assassin to this jumble of people at close range? How could anyone with a gun get right to him? What kind of law is this in Dallas? Who on earth did it? Why?

And as we heard some of the answers, incredulity was supplanted by disgust and fury, and these in turn by a sense of the insanely grotesque: a strip-tease proprietor, a small-time crook, had deprived the American people and the accused murderer of their President of justice on the actual premises of law: police headquarters. Then outrage took over again: outrage at the enormity of the act, at violence so close to the surface, at the boundless bungling of those fat Texas police. It was in relief that we came back to the President's body and the muffled drums. Sorrow, however vast, was better than outrage. That could wait till later.

By Monday a great silence had settled over the nation as the last act of the tragedy was played. I had watched the leaders of the nations of the world arrive the night before at Dulles Airport as a drawn Dean Rusk, waiting and pacing, greeted each in turn: the towering President de Gaulle, the small Asians and Africans, the tall Nordic princes, the Arabs and the Israelis, the Italians and the Dutch. Now I watched them assemble at the White House for that walk to the Cathedral of St. Matthew.

Now, in the brilliant cold November light, they gathered behind the President's wife and the President's two brothers who once more were behind the caisson bearing the President's body and the fretting Blackjack and the seven gray horses. You could see her features under the heavy black veil only enough to know that they were still composed; her arms hung straight at her sides. Robert Kennedy's face bore, as always during the four long days, the bleakness of devastation together with, it seemed to me, a mighty anger.

Slowly the cortege and the leaders of the nations walked in the winter sun to the Cathedral, and then we—all of us again —were in the church. Millions, I am sure, were deeply moved by what transpired there. Unhappily I felt Cardinal Cushing not as an assuager of my grief but as an intruder into it: the grating cadences of his loud voice, the harshness of his Latin and English speech, took from the service much that would have been beautiful. I told myself that this old man was a lifelong friend of the President and his family, that if they loved him there was much to love, and that his sorrow was boundless. But

But Will It Sell?

I wanted his talking to end in the church as I wanted it to end later at Arlington, and as, so few years ago, I wanted it to come to an end at the inauguration of the man he now mourned. The silence was the balm.

And now we went with the President to Arlington; every step of the way. The streets and bridges of the capital were beautiful, the approach to Arlington a fitting entry to peace, the heroes waiting under their headstones to be joined by one of their company.

We heard the skirl of bagpipes, we walked close to the grave, we watched the honor guard take the flag from the casket and hold it taut between them, we saw the standing mourners still as stone. Then we saw the flag folded over and over and placed in the hands of Jacqueline Kennedy. And with tears now uncontainable we heard the high and lonely bugle notes of taps.

The light had gone out; the lights were lit; not only on the grave of the murdered President but in the halls of state where the new President, only hours later, received the leaders with whom, from this moment on, he would have to treat.

Only this scene, a sort of social sarabande unreal in its conventionality, could have finally stemmed our tears and bridged the chasm between death and life. Here was the big new President pumping hand after hand, smiling and nodding; here were, except for De Gaulle, much smaller men trying to impress themselves on the mind of the new executive; here were old allies and old adversaries and the new men of new countries coming to pay court in the hopes of being courted, anxious to tell their people what this new leader was like; how he looked and talked, how he behaved to them.

And then, finally, there were the lights in the private apartments of the White House; and when we saw these we turned the set off and left Mrs. John F. Kennedy to the protective cover of darkness, and ourselves—the millions and millions of us—to the respite denied her.

4: Controverse

PREFACE
VERSE

PREFACE

GLANCING AT A NEWSPAPER REVIEW of the work of several poets not long ago, my eye was abruptly arrested by the following line: "Light verse is for desperate people."

As a far from desperate but now affronted practitioner of light verse, I reread the paragraph that preceded it. In it, the reviewer commented that Mr. John Updike was one of the cleverest of the *New Yorker* verse writers and could write amusingly about a washing machine, a stanza about which he quoted.

"My objection to this kind of writing," said the reviewer, "is that it is a waste of time. It is an appalling thought that for many people who do get round to reading poetry now and then, this is the sort of poetry they like."

Appalling? I am happily not alone in being grateful to any poet, however shallow, who not only permits me to understand what he is saying but says it with skill and wit and gaiety. I don't care if he writes about a car, a woman or a platypus, so long as his eye is fresh, his rhythm lively, and his rhyming deft. A good word game can tease and delight more than a shrouded riddle of symbols, and a well-turned couplet often say more than a solemn column.

And then, whose time is wasted? The writer's? Anything that gives pleasure surely is born of pleasure, and it is a great satisfaction to a poet to seal the right fly in the right shape of amber. As for the reader, something that takes no time wastes no time: light verse is a read-and-run sport.

Nor does a frivolous form necessarily enclose a frivolous thought. Wit has a deadly aim and it is possible to prick a large pretense with a small pin. Intellectuals are prone to believe that you can only treat of serious things in a serious way. And not only intellectuals: It is an American custom to distrust wit and confuse the unserious with the insincere. Adlai Stevenson can testify eloquently to this attitude, which explains also why most political speeches are both mirthless and dull. Laughs are for comics only, and the test of sincerity is the weight of the platitude.

Anyway, some of us cannot resist unserious verse as a way of saying, sometimes with the utmost gravity, what we feel about certain things—sad, funny, or catastrophic. It is given to very few to be great poets; the rest of us must be content to sing in our small voices in our own way. I for one have no illusions about the importance of the verse I write. At its best it may be brushed by the wings of poetry; sometimes it is merely neat and clever; often it is little more than doggerel. Most of it was triggered off by news items and quotes, usually in the back pages of the newspapers.

But will it sell? Even the best poetry has a limited audience, and light verse is popular only if the foil is rubber-tipped. Mine is not.

Yet if in spite of the naked point these verses should succeed in giving you any pleasure, at any level, it is merely a reflection of my own in producing it. And it says things I wouldn't know how to say in prose.

146

VERSE

FOLKLORE, U.S.

CHILDREN'S GIFT LIST

*A logless log cabin . . . is
marked at $495. . . . Extras . . .
are the front veranda, at $65,
and the lookout tower for spot-
ting Indians, at $48.*

Just a simple rustic pad
For a simple little lad
From a simple-minded Dad
Yearly used to being had.

*Little girls need no longer
feel that playing with dolls is a
one-way proposition. 'Kissy,'
for instance, will kiss back in-
definitely, so long as her arms
are drawn together.*

Perfect for your favorite missy
Is the little nympho Kissy.
Keep her well away from sonny
Lest he take her for his Bunny.

147

*"Morticia," a black-gowned
Charles Addams doll with
chalk-white face . . . just the
Christmas gift for the little girl
who has everything.*

> Scary Christmas, dear Patricia,
> From the sinister Morticia.
> See directions, if you break her:
> How to Be an Undertaker.

WATCH THAT MUSE

*Arnold Mitchell, an econo-
mist, said his research had
shown him that there are more
piano players than fishermen
and as many painters as hunt-
ers.*

> Culture, stay thy fearful hand!
> The sound of stilly waters
> Is infinitely sweeter than
> The practicing of daughters,
>
> And any harm that hunters do
> Is mild when you envision
> The massacres that oft ensue
> From paint-on-paint collision.
>
> So heed our warning, gentle muse,
> Or you may overdo it:
> When culture is too common, who's
> Inspired to pursue it?

THE AMERICAN DREAM

*Underlying all these [pro-
grams for youth] as both pre-
ventive and cure is a happy*

148

family; one that finds its great-
est enjoyment in such things as
the family picnic, the "cookout"
or home movies. . . . We must
see to it that our children grow
up in a climate that encourages
the dignity of man.
    —President Eisenhower

Bring the charcoal for the grill,
    Don't forget the mayonnaise,
Roast the wienies with a will,
    Daddy's got himself a raise.

Momma's got herself a brood
    Battened on a barbecue,
Happiness is fun and food
    Kodachromed for later view.

Pass the mustard, pass the can,
    Grampa's set the nation's goal:
Spread the dignity of man
    Lightly on a toasted roll.

JUKE BOX

Put a quarter in a slot,
What've you got?
    Rock 'n' roll, lost soul,
    Demon whine, moonshine,
    June moon, high croon,
    Down beat, dog in heat,
    Hot blues, bad news,
And a million bucks for a gangster.

Put a quarter in a slot,
What've you got?
    Dull throb, dazed slob,

Low hum, lower bum,
Pop tune, big goon,
Young punk, old drunk,
Spent nights, colored lights,
And a million bucks for a gangster.

FOLK LAW

Folk Singers Riot in Wash-
ington Sq. Ten Arrested, Sev-
eral Hurt as Musicians and
Followers Protest City's Ban.

Black is the color of my true love's hair
    And black is the heart of a city
That threatens my right in a public square
    To strum a guitar to a ditty.

Blue is the uniform my true foe wears
    And black is the club he is swinging—
The cop gets his pay-off and nobody cares
    But the singer is picked up for singing.

THE PAMPERED

The television set, the mov-
ies and the myriad conveniences
and distractions of modern life
all lure our young people away
from the strenuous physical ac-
tivity which is the basis of fit-
ness in youth and in later life.
—President John F. Kennedy

Junior needs the car tonight
(His date's a mile away).
Sister's staying home from school
(It's going to snow today).

Billy's sprawling by the set,
Shirley's by the phone,
Eddie's on his second Coke,
Jean, her second cone.

Soft and white the daily bread,
Crustless for our youth,
Gooey-smooth the caramel
For the tender tooth.

Sheltered from the elements,
Shielded from the air,
Watch them palely loitering
On sofa, bed, and chair:

Children of a way of life,
American, unique,
Where Comfort is bequeathing them
The freedom to be weak.

LOOPHOLE

*Two psychiatrists were de-
nied tax deductions for getting
psychoanalyzed. . . . Under
the tax law, education ex-
penses are deductible when intended to improve one's skills
in an existing job, but not to
prepare for a better one.*

Can a painter who is painted claim deductions?
Can seducers who'er seduced deduct seductions?
Can a writer, written of, write off this writing
As a necessary lesson in backbiting?

Can a preacher who is preached at claim exemption
For thus furthering his practice of redemption?

How infinitely logical, what fun to
Deduct in kind for what one has been done to!

THIS LITTLE PIGGIE

*How to tell when you've
"arrived" . . . When you and
the maître d' discuss the Market before the Menu.*—Adv.

I've made it, I've made it!
I gave Emile
A tip on the market, a sure-fire deal,
And after he thanked me, he said would I care
For his very superlative moules marinieres?

I've made it, I've made it!
Emile told me
Of a hint he had heard about L.F. and E.,
And after I thanked him, I said I'd prefer
Their really delectable cervelles au beurre!

DANGER FROM WITHIN

*D.A.R. Facing Uprising by
Anti-Isolationist Wing*

Strip off the orchids, dames, and buckle on
The ample breastplates of your ignorance—
The traitors move against you, softly now
In Mayflower corridors, and whisper treason.
So hurry: gird, raise high the ancestral lance
And march against the champions of reason,
While cherry blossoms fall and people smile
At the recurrence of the silly season.

BLIGHT ON BLIGHT

Young painters picketed the Museum of Modern Art . . . to protest its preference for abstract works.

Hear the rebels giving tongue,
Painters panting to be hung,
Turning worms against the blight
Of black on black and white on white,
Against the splash, against the dribble,
Against the psychopathic scribble;
Demanding space upon the wall
For something less conventional.

WASTED RESOURCE

Specially designed deck scows carrying spectacular outdoor advertising signs will soon begin circling New York on the Hudson and East Rivers . . . the signs will be viewed by millions of motorists on New York's two major highways . . . [and by] people on ferries and in offices and residential buildings.—A press release.

There was something wrong with the rivers—
They carried boats to the sea;
They carried cargoes in covered holds
And the freight of mystery.

There was something wrong with the rivers—
There was nothing at all to see
But the gliding waters, tankers, tugs
In the tide of destiny.

There was something wrong with the rivers,
They had nothing at all to sell—
But now they will shine with the huckster's sign,
And all is well.

TIME, GENTLEMEN, PLEASE

*Americans Found to Lack
Leisure; Philosopher Says They
Keep Too Busy During Time
Spent Off the Job.*

Lie down and listen to the crabgrass grow,
The faucet leak, and learn to leave them so.
Feel how the breezes play about your hair
And sunlight settles on your breathing skin.
What else can matter but the drifting glance
On dragonfly or sudden shadow there
Of swans aloft and the whiffle of their wings
On air to other ponds? Nothing but this:
To see, to wonder, to receive, to feel
What lies in the circle of your singleness.
Think idly of a woman or a verse
Or bees or vapor trails or why the birds
Are still at noon. Yourself, be still—
There is no living when you're nagging time
And stunting every second with your will.
You work for this: to be the sovereign
Of what you slave to have—not
Slave.

THE CARDS

It comes, it comes, the blizzard of December,
The great white flakes that sift along the floor,
Settle on tables, mantles, shelves; pile
In bowls, cling on screens, flutter
On ribbons, drift beneath the door; the flakes

Heavy as guilt, light as love, soft
As memory. They come, the photographs of children
Year after year, serene, shining, growing,
The pride of families—"Behold our brood!" They come:
The engravings of naval battles or Dickens dinners
From England; the simpering tinted lovers behind roses
From wags in Europe; the chaste expensive greetings
From correct conservatives; the planes embossed
On heavy foil or the hard New York skyline
From business names; the little medieval woodcuts from the
    Museum
And modest friends; the richly reproduced
Religious paintings from the richer ones
Partial to art if not to liturgy. They come,
They come: the glitter-sprinkled snow
From Anna, who cleans; the wavering drawing of Madonna and
    Child
From the niece with talent and feeling; the hung-over
Sick-joke Santa from a boy at school; the legends of peace
In a dozen languages from the U.N. They come, they come,
The cats from lovers of cats, the dogs from dog lovers,
The abstractions from intellectuals abreast with the times
And above the season; the sleighs and holly berries
From old friends in the country and in the past. They come,
They come; with names printed (Miss Jones, order six hundred)
    or names scrawled,
They come with "love" inserted, or nothing; from far and near,
Duty or impulse; cold as habit, warm as love, dry
As experience. It comes, the December blizzard; instiller of guilt,
Prodder of memory, opener of heart; nuisance, rite,
.Waste, pleasure, compulsion; and millions of dollars
For makers of greeting cards. It comes;
It goes.

OF WAR, HOT AND COLD

CHICKEN

Does the world think Americans are afraid of nuclear war and death? The true Americans are not.—Adv.

I'm not a true American,
I fear a nuclear war,
I fear the death of all of us,
I fear the fearless more:

I fear the true Americans
Who do not fear a war,
Who have not taught themselves to know
What human life is for.

I'm not a true American,
I'd rather live to see
The most exasperating peace
Than simply not to Be.

CUBA, '61

Companion Fear is at my side,
I cannot make him leave,
He whispers horror in my ear,
He twitches at my sleeve.

He presses down upon my heart,
He catches at my breath,
He does not need to put in words
The hovering of death.

Companion Fear is at my side,
I cannot make him go,
For we are bound in common dread
Of what we do not know.

ICECAPADE

*"Large-scale weather control
techniques might be used . . .
to bring a new 'ice age' upon
the enemy," Admiral [William
F.] Raborn suggested.*

How peaceable the frozen enemy,
Glittering apex of the coldest war!
The Kremlin jeweled in ice, the hordes at last
Stopped in their shuffling, the Praesidium
A gelid waxworks, all the invincible
Machines ice-bound! Now all can see
The Frigor Mortis of a bad idea
Caught in the act—in aspic—prison in prism—
As intricate, overworked as any
Fabergé of the Czars, and equally
Outdated: Communism.

LINES ADDED TO FU HSUAN (died 278)

*Radio Peiping has warned
that the population in Sinkiang
Province, in northwest China,
is threatened by "a dense and
poisonous radioactive fallout"
coming from the Soviet
Union. . . .*

"A gentle wind fans the calm night:
A bright moon shines on the high tower.
A voice whispers, but no one answers when I call:
A shadow stirs, but no one comes when I beckon."

157

I breathe and poison fills my lungs—
The moon is darkened and a gray rain falls:
A greeting, O my brothers, from our friends.

STOCK PILE

What trireme in Phoenician waters bore
A cargo lovelier on the tongue? "Beryllium,
Agar, asbestos, opium," should be sung
To the purling of oars. Molybdenum,
Nickel and quinine, talc, feathers and down—
The smooth and bitter, powdery and bright,
The viscous—castor oil, the sapphire—hard
And brilliant as the diamond dies.
And here the lovely queens with streaming hair:
Vanadium, Zirconium—of where?
No matter; words are worlds. Agar, beryllium,
Sapphire, feathers and down—too lovely for
The ugly hoard of war.

SWASTIKA

What can erase
This thing from the scrawled
Walls of the mind; exterminate
This spider from the infested conscience? It hooks
Convulsively on the memory of man: the obscene
Insignia of hate. It mates and spawns
In every season and climate, crawls
On the faces of Nations. What
Can kill it but implacable
Wrath?

THE REFUGEES

They are all the same, these people, no matter where
They flee, no matter what
Set them to shuffling with their last few things

158

On the roads of the world. A powerful lens would show
These clots and clusters of the lost, these scribbles moving
Across the invisible lines that separate
One nation from the next, one day from another,
The known from the not yet known. They are all the same,
These people; stirring the conscience for a while,
And shame, and then
Nothing.

SPACE

REQUIESCAT IN ORBITUM

Space "burial" problems are probed by Aerojet-General scientists. They conclude the best solution on a multi-crewed deep space mission would be a "space version of burial at sea." A dead astronaut "should be simply pushed into space where his body would vanish into the vastness."

Push me simply into space
    And leave me on my way
Running an immortal race
    With night and day.

Then I would be free at last,
    A particle of air,
Worm and fire bypassed
    And coffin bare.

Whiter than a sailor's bone
    Washed in the deep,
I with my starry own
    Would vigil keep.

NOVITIATES

Shortage of Rabbis is Called Acute. Dearth of Priests Deplored in Rome (Separate headlines, same day, same paper.)

Rabbi shortage called acute,
  Dearth of priests deplored in Rome. . . .
Searching for the absolute,
  Looking for the spirit's home,
Young men walk in other ways,
  Seek it in another place,
Learning other words to praise
  His inalterable grace.
Not for some the solemn robe
  Nor the litany of prayer,
They salute the shining globe
  With the lexicon of air,
Finding in their starry search
  In the ecstasies of space,
More than synagogue or church
  Tell them of the spirit's place.

GROUNDED

Mrs. Sara Bartholomae, Los Angeles, announced plans to build $1,000,000 public chapel in shape of Mercury capsule to commemorate John Glenn's space flight.—Bulletin of the American Association of Fund Raising Counsel.

All systems Go, all circuits A.O.K.,
Encapsulated now, come let us pray,
And lying weightless in our contour chair,
Repeat as one this astronautic prayer:
That all these men who hurtle into space

May never have to see this costly place,
Or know—who measured the celestial girth—
The hideous follies of abandoned Earth.

MESSAGE

*It's only a little bit of wax
. . . but it rode to earth from
outer space in a meteorite and
three scientists said it brought
this message: There is life in
the universe other than that on
earth.*

It's only a little bit of wax
    That fell from a piece of sky,
But it says, as sure as your income tax:
    Here too live I.

It's only a hydrocarbon trace
    As thin as an apple skin,
As loud as a voice from outer space:
    We are, have been.

POLITICKING

AFTER ELECTIONS

Half of the people will be low,
    Half of the people high;
The wind of change is bound to blow
    Whether they beam or sigh.

All of the speeches, all the claims
    Count for nothing now.
People have had their fill of Aims;
    They wait for When and How.

All of the world is waiting too
With fearful breath to see
Whether we know what we must do
And are as we must be.

TV LESSON

*The experts instructed the
politicians . . . in the techniques
of dressing, talking, gesturing,
and looking sincere. . . .*

Look the camera in the eye,
Keep the chin-line firm,
Sit with nonchalance and try
Not to shift or squirm.

When you speak of origins,
Family, or life,
Cultivate the boyish grin
That won your girlish wife.

Let the mouth be grim and straight
When you talk of prayer,
Morality, the Soviet State,
And Freedom Everywhere.

Never rise above your kind
Even if you could:
To have an ordinary mind
Is for the common good.

All this you should know by now,
The model has been clear:
It's never what you say, but how
You make it sound sincere.

SCANDAL

With a jubilant shout
The party that's out
Discovers the sin
Of the party that's in.
Faces are red,
Bodies are dead,
And there's something very
Rotten in cotton.

The party that's out
Forgets about
The things it did,
Identical (id.),
When it was in.
They were no sin,
Just errors of judgment—
Sad, not bad.

The party that's out,
Beyond a doubt,
Paid no penny
For anything any-
body could do
To help it through.
Did it stoop to
Fraud? Good Lawd!

CAMPAIGN

According to the opposition
The country's heading for perdition—
How odd that only half the nation
Can hold the key to its salvation!

FAUNA

ET TU, BRUTE

Arteriosclerosis in Animals and Birds is up Tenfold—"Social Pressure" Cited.

If the bellbird is bats and the gnu is gnurotic,
   If the crocodile's crocked in his pool,
If the buffalo's bushed and the pseal is psychotic
   And the potto's beginning to pule,

It's the faces, the faces, from morning till night,
   The faces outside of the cage,
It's the terrible faces forever in sight
   That accelerate animal age;

That wrinkle the wrhino and cripple the crow
   And tire the testy toucan,
For there's nothing that wears out an animal so
   As the bestial stare of a man.

BEE LINE

Congress was told today that it is dangerous for American honeybees to associate with foreign honeybees.

Ah love, how sweet
To pollinate
Across the sea!

Your foreign fuzz
And alien buzz
Enchanted me!

164

But now it seems
Our honeyed dreams
Can be no more—

A cruel state
Decrees I mate
The bee next door.

WAKE UP AND READ

*Air Force scientists have
been teaching octopuses to
"read."*

Down on the sea bed, a book in every arm,
See the giant cephalopods in literacy's charm;
Publishers are jubilant, for now at least they know
Each volume will sell eight-fold (or squid pro quo).

OF LIFE AND DEATH

IN MEMORY

(Eleanor Roosevelt)

Her enemies were small: the shriveled ones
Who find in any largeness of the heart
Folly or danger. But the multitude
Gave back to her what she held out to them:
The steady glow of love, the succoring hand,
The enlightened eye of reason. So, now ends
The amazing cycle: humble, lonely girl
To great and humble woman; and the world,
Claiming and losing her,
Is lonelier.

VILLA LA PAUSA

(Winston Churchill)

Thus would he paint it: walls of white and roof
Red-tiled and shutters lavender, not closed
But wide to the incredible blue sea.
And he would paint the olives and the firs
And the hot flowers shimmering in light
No English sun bestows. This Englishman
Has been the flame himself. What he has warmed
Has been the world. And when the heat is gone
The world will shrivel. Think of him like this:
The sailor resting, part of sea and sky
And all the simple marvels of an earth
Which gave this great soul birth.

REJECTION

*The familiar words in the
Twenty-third psalm "the valley
of the shadow of death" have
been altered to "the darkest
valley" in the proposed new
Psalter for the Church of England.*

No, it won't do. I happen to know the place:
Sunny and fair, but down in the deepest gorge,
In silence, something passes between the sun
And me: a wing, a cloud, a breath
That chokes my own. I know this valley well,
I know this thing to be the shadow of death.

EXIT VISA

And armless babies still
May not be all. What price tranquility per pill? Not much:
Blue, yellow, pink, red, brown, the little round
Pellet of peace resolves so many things,

Muffles the hammering of pain, the ping of fear,
The pang of conscience. Brings
A fluid rest like the prenatal sac. But brings
What else? What new monstrosity
Of mind or soul long after? What despair,
What malady of flesh? Who knows, who knows
But that release is dearly bought when bought
Rather than won in solitary war
On the darkest nights. There is a trick in ease;
The quick escape, unfought for, should suffice
To alarm the mind. But still, flesh, mind
Crave the relief, now, soon—
Whether from terrors of the spirit or of this earth
To flee, to drown; even to fly
To the moon.

KINZUA DAM

*Seneca Ceremony Mourns
Land Taken by U.S. Despite
Treaty.*

Land, my land!
    I will go up to the mountains
And there I will watch the waters
Thundering over my valleys
And there will I lament them;
Crying,
    O my land!
What is my life to me, now you are
        departed?

Home, my home!
    Promised to us forever,
Sworn in the white man's treaty
Always to be our dwelling;

Now,
　　O my land,
　　A Lake of Perfidy. I weep for my
　　　betrayers.

IN OTHER PARTS

SUMMER THOUGHTS OF A SNOB

Now that the Off is Beaten Track, preserve me from
Summer in Europe. I have no wish to go
Where the rest are going: Bill, Edie, Ed, the man who does my
　　hair,
Miss P. in Filing, the Marches with their young,
The folk from Winnetka, Purple Springs, Wahooskie,
A million Americans bound for the lovely places
I once saw hearing only a different tongue and seeing
Strange people and smelling and tasting newly every day,
Strange to myself as well as strange to others.

Preserve me now
From a Europe tailored to our aseptic tastes, with Haig and Haig
Handy in every wineshop in every province
And Cokes all over; and in some mountain town
Drene, Gleem and Kleenex, Pond's, Band-Aid and Lux
Ready on shelves for timid modern women,
And every village geared to childish lips
With franks and hamburgers and banana splits
Where cheese and wine once warmed the exploring tongue.

Preserve me from One World, One Way, Our Way
Prevailing, the common coinage of the kingdom of comfort
Dispelling difference. And save me from seeing
"David" in Florence surrounded by my kind,
However happy, humble, decent and generous:

The rumpled men, shirt open, the straps of gear
Dragging their Dacron shoulders down, their slackened mouths
Loose-hung. Preserve me from their wives,
Eager in cottons, pixie-glasses bright,
Telling their families shrilly where to look.
Preserve me from their young—the pretty, precocious
Girls, kid-brother boys
Fat-buttocked in their jeans, the slouching youths
Looking for Bardot, bored with the Bargello.

Preserve me too
From all my sophisticated friends who know just where
To eat, sleep, drive, buy charming little things
At next to nothing. Let them go, I say,
And blessings on them for all the joys they reap.
I will stay here. The places in their season
Are for too many. Antibes, the Costa Brava,
Rome, Venice, Capri, Ischia, all those places
Eye-worn, herd-trodden, overused, un-strange,
Vacation-weary. I do not want those beaches
Padded with basting flesh, the *trattorias*
Loud with American cries, while waiters' eyes
Glisten derisively, their palms outstretched
For the preposterous overtip.

Preserve me too
From the Germans and English in Italy and France
And the French in France, high-voiced in penury
On their paid holidays. All men are equal
To see all things, and this is fine for them, but I
Prefer the priority of singleness
In seeing. To be the one
Stranger before the undiscovered sight, the house or hill
None else is seeing now. And if this means
Choosing the bitter climates of the year,
The shrouded sun, cold rooms, deserted streets,

And worst of all, places still poor in plumbing—
Tell no one else; but I, a snob,
Am coming.

THE RUBAIYAT OF OMAR HILTON

*Now, in 1963, the minarets
of Iran and the Acropolis of
Greece look out on two wonders of the modern world . . .
History meets tomorrow with
two new Hilton Hotels.*—Adv.

The moving Builder builds, and having built
Moves on; the Milk (or rather Concrete) spilt,
    The kinship claimed with an offended Past
That watches Profit grow and Beauty wilt.

Yesterday this day's Madness did prepare:
Tomorrow's Hostel and the People there,
    Who may know Whence they came, but hardly Why—
Except to Drink and Sleep and Sit and Stare.

A moment's Halt, a momentary Taste
Of Culture from the Well among the Waste,
    And lo—the tourist Caravan has reached
The Nothing it set out from, Hilton-based.

UHURU

*Does it come wrapped in
paper and do we go to the bank
and get it? Lulua tribesmen
asked an American missionary
. . . Independence is not easily
grasped by the Congolese.*

Bongo, bongo, drums of the Congo,
Come to the Great Unwrapping—
Tear off the paper and pull off the string,

170

Open it up and grasp the Thing,
Shiny freedom and golden ease,
Raise your head and do as you please,
Yours to have and yours to hold,
Never more doing as you've been told,
A little more beer, a little more salt,
Game for the killing and none to halt.

Bongo, bongo, drums of the Congo,
Open the package with care—
Trial and trouble are wrapped in there,
And the hasty grab of the hidden crown
Can summon the evil spirits down:
Kindred bathed in the blood of blame,
Meat today, but the end of game,
Famine after the sudden fill,
And liberty still beyond the hill.

WHITE AFRICA

The hand is itching for the whip,
The forearm for the blow,
The curse is trembling on the lip
But must unuttered go,
While dead colonials soundlessly
Cry out in vindication, "See
What happens when you set
    them free?"

COW COUNTRY

The Swiss have Alps, the Swiss have cows,
    The Swiss have trousered gloaters
In men who've voted that their fraus
    May not be women voters.

UNCLASSIFIED

HELPMEET

A British scientist is working on a robot which may take over a housewife's routine. "Eventually . . . I hope there will be a robot housemaid about as intelligent as a monkey and costing the same as a small auto."

Minnie was a honey with an automatic brain,
She knew just when to polish and put Drano down the drain,
She'd dolly from the washer to the oven and the sink
Or mix a fine Martini which she never had to drink
She never talked or balked or whined or asked to be admired,
But did, while there was juice in her, whatever was required.
Now Minnie was created to emancipate a wife
From all the weary nuisances that clutter up her life,
But once the men could buy her and install her in the home,
A wife became redundant and the males began to roam
In search of something brighter and more cuddlesome than she,
Less costly than a little car, but just as fancy free.
So, housewives, ponder carefully before you start to pray
For Minnie's consummation: you may learn to rue the day.

THIS MAY HURT A LITTLE

A Tucson dentist broke two drills and spent several hours grinding away before completing an extraction Sunday. The patient was a Titan 2 intercontinental ballistic missile. A draft pin had snapped and no machine shop in Tucson had the delicate instrument required for removal of the pin.

From now on, NASA-honey, this'll
Bind me emotionally to a missile:

To think an object—tiny, dental—
Can be so hugely instrumental,
And that such human tortures smite an
Organism like the Titan!

AIM TO PLEASE

*Archery "Lanes" Hope to
Rival Bowling With Automated
Targets—Push-Button Device
Returns Arrows, Target to
Fans.*

I shot an arrow in the air,
It hit a target over there,
I pressed a button where I stood
And pitied sorry Robin Hood,
Who had to walk to what he hit
To get his arrow out of it.

WATER BABY

*Two leading scientists said
today that life might have
begun ashore, rather than at
sea, as has been supposed.*

No, gentlemen, you can't do that to me—
I who remember crawling from the sea
And growing limbs and lungs so that in time
I could arise from the primordial slime!
You say I must renounce my ancient mother,
I who embrace the porpoise as my brother
And find in every blue and briny motion
The healing fluid of my source, the ocean.
Ah no. My every dream is born at sea,
I'll not accept this new maternity,
Standing, I fear, irrevocably pat
With those who thundered that the world was flat!

173

ISLAND

(By sea mail from the Bahamas)

What shall I send from a reef of coral
A thousand leagues from pressure and print?
Of heavy times and the titan quarrel
Never a shadow and no hint.

Never a shadow other than palm
Bending over a blinding beach,
Nothing but iridescent calm
Far and blue as the eye can reach.

What can I rhyme of man's commotion,
How can I point a potent moral,
When all I know is the sound of ocean
Lapping over a reef of coral?

5: *The Culture Bit*

PREFACE

EVERY WRITER has a set of obsessions: recurring themes which he feels compelled to express in different ways at different times.

One of mine is the business of standards: how do you know what's good? How do you know what's right? How *do* you?

I would doubt whether there has been any time when a society was provided with fewer charts to the regions of behavior, judgment, and choice than now. The old signposts have been taken down and the new ones say "Anything Goes" or "It's a Matter of Taste." Or people who claim to know the forests intimately lead you through the thickets of fashion telling you, "Follow us: This is the way."

But nobody gives you a compass, because compasses, we are told, are obsolete. True North is where anyone wants to go. Truth, in fact, is where you find it: a private enterprise.

But Will It Sell?

So here we are, confronted with new writing, new painting, new theatre, new architecture, and new behavoir, with no way to measure it except in terms of success and popularity and even these often inflated far beyond their reality by the techniques of press agentry and clique support.

What we have arrived at, I think, is a kind of anarchy. Whether it is affluent boys who break up the house of their hosts, or painters who smash space, or writers who fragment language, the destruction of existing forms has left a void more often than it has replaced them with a new order. Continuity, the solace of man, has been deliberately fractured, as windows are smashed, by the attention getters and the seekers—infantile and primitive —of instant gratification. (Instant art, instant sex, instant fame— it doesn't matter what you want so long as you get it now.) How dismiss these for what they are and still recognize the long-distance runners, the torch bearers, the real inheritors and innovators?

Where is the cultural dowser, divining the true creative springs?

I don't know. But we sorely need one: guide, compass, chart, call it what you will, to make at least a little sense out of what is close to chaos. Without it, culture is a word and not a condition.

The piece that follows next was originally a speech given to journalism students at Marquette University in which I tried to define the responsibility of the press to the arts. If it will help future arbiters to withhold the word "art" from such idiocies and pretensions as Pop Art and crushed car fenders, it will have served some purpose.

HOW DO YOU KNOW
IT'S GOOD?

SUPPOSE THERE WERE NO CRITICS to tell
us how to react to a picture, a play, or a new composition of
music. Suppose we wandered innocent as the dawn into an art
exhibition of unsigned paintings. By what standards, by what
values would we decide whether they were good or bad, talented
or untalented, successes or failures? How can we ever know
that what we think is right?

For the last fifteen or twenty years the fashion in criticism
or appreciation of the arts has been to deny the existence of
any valid criteria and to make the words "good" or "bad" irrelevant, immaterial, and inapplicable. There is no such thing,
we are told, as a set of standards, first acquired through experience and knowledge and later imposed on the subject under
discussion. This has been a popular approach, for it relieves the
critic of the responsibility of judgment and the public of the
necessity of knowledge. It pleases those resentful of disciplines,
it flatters the empty-minded by calling them open-minded, it
comforts the confused. Under the banner of democracy and
the kind of equality which our forefathers did *not* mean, it says,
in effect, "Who are you to tell us what is good or bad?" This
is the same cry used so long and so effectively by the producers
of mass media who insist that it is the public, not they, who
decides what it wants to hear and see, and that for a critic to
say that *this* program is bad and *this* program is good is purely
a reflection of personal taste. Nobody recently has expressed

179

this philosophy more succinctly than Dr. Frank Stanton, the highly intelligent president of CBS television. At a hearing before the Federal Communications Commission, this phrase escaped him under questioning: "One man's mediocrity is another man's good program."

There is no better way of saying "No values are absolute." There is another important aspect to this philosophy of *laissez faire:* It is the fear, in all observers of all forms of art, of guessing wrong. This fear is well come by, for who has not heard of the contemporary outcries against artists who later were called great? Every age has its arbiters who do not grow with their times, who cannot tell evolution from revolution or the difference between frivolous faddism, amateurish experimentation, and profound and necessary change. Who wants to be caught *flagrante delicto* with an error of judgment as serious as this? It is far safer, and certainly easier, to look at a picture or a play or a poem and to say "This is hard to understand, but it may be good," or simply to welcome it as a new form. The word "new"—in our country especially—has magical connotations. What is new must be good; what is old is probably bad. And if a critic can describe the new in language that nobody can understand, he's safer still. If he has mastered the art of saying nothing with exquisite complexity, nobody can quote him later as saying anything.

But all these, I maintain, are forms of abdication from the responsibility of judgment. In creating, the artist commits himself; in appreciating, you have a commitment of your own. For after all, it is the audience which makes the arts. A climate of appreciation is essential to its flowering, and the higher the expectations of the public, the better the performance of the artist. Conversely, only a public ill-served by its critics could have accepted as art and as literature so much in these last years that has been neither. If anything goes, everything goes; and at the bottom of the junkpile lie the discarded standards too.

But what are these standards? How do you get them? How

do you know they're the right ones? How can you make a clear pattern out of so many intangibles, including that greatest one, the very private I?

Well for one thing, it's fairly obvious that the more you read and see and hear, the more equipped you'll be to practice that art of association which is at the basis of all understanding and judgment. The more you live and the more you look, the more aware you are of a consistent pattern—as universal as the stars, as the tides, as breathing, as night and day—underlying everything. I would call this pattern and this rhythm an order. Not order—*an* order. Within it exists an incredible diversity of forms. Without it lies chaos. I would further call this order—this incredible diversity held within one pattern—health. And I would call chaos—the wild cells of destruction—sickness. It is in the end up to you to distinguish between the diversity that is health and the chaos that is sickness, and you can't do this without a process of association that can link a bar of Mozart with the corner of a Vermeer painting, or a Stravinsky score with a Picasso abstraction; or that can relate an aggressive act with a Franz Kline painting and a fit of coughing with a John Cage composition.

There is no accident in the fact that certain expressions of art live for all time and that others die with the moment, and although you may not always define the reasons, you can ask the questions. What does an artist say that is timeless; how does he say it? How much is fashion, how much is merely reflection? Why is Sir Walter Scott so hard to read now, and Jane Austen not? Why is baroque right for one age and too effulgent for another?

Can a standard of craftsmanship apply to art of all ages, or does each have its own, and different, definitions? You may have been aware, inadvertently, that craftsmanship has become a dirty word these years because, again, it implies standards—something done well or done badly. The result of this convenient avoidance is a plenitude of actors who can't project their voices, singers who can't phrase their songs, poets who can't communicate emotion, and writers who have no vocabulary —not to speak of painters who can't draw. The dogma now is that craftsmanship gets in the way of expression. You can do better if you don't know *how* you do it, let alone *what* you're doing.

I think it is time you helped reverse this trend by trying to rediscover craft: the command of the chosen instrument, whether it is a brush, a word, or a voice. When you begin to detect the difference between freedom and sloppiness, between serious experimentation and egotherapy, between skill and slickness, between strength and violence, you are on your way to separating the sheep from the goats, a form of segregation denied us for quite a while. All you need to restore it is a small bundle of standards and a Geiger counter that detects fraud, and we might begin our tour of the arts in an area where both are urgently needed: contemporary painting.

I don't know what's worse: to have to look at acres of bad art to find the little good, or to read what the critics say about it all. In no other field of expression has so much double-talk flourished, so much confusion prevailed, and so much nonsense been circulated: further evidence of the close interdependence between the arts and the critical climate they inhabit. It will be my pleasure to share with you some of this double-talk so typical of our times.

Item one: preface for a catalogue of an abstract painter:

"Time-bound meditation experiencing a life; sincere with plastic piety at the threshold of hallowed arcana; a striving for pure ideation giving shape to inner drive; formalized patterns where neural balances reach a fiction." End of quote. Know what this artist paints like now?

Item two: a review in the *Art News:*

". . . a weird and disparate assortment of material, but the monstrosity which bloomed into his most recent cancer of aggregations is present in some form everywhere. . . ." Then, later, "A gluttony of things and processes terminated by a glorious constipation."

The Culture Bit

Item three, same magazine, review of an artist who welds automobile fragments into abstract shapes:

"Each fragment . . . is made an extreme of human exasperation, torn at and fought all the way, and has its rightness of form as if by accident. *Any technique that requires order or discipline would just be the human ego.* No, these must be egoless, uncontrolled, undesigned and different enough to give you a bang—fifty miles an hour around a telephone pole. . . ."

"Any technique that requires order of discipline would just be the human ego." What does he mean—"just be"? What are they really talking about? Is this journalism? Is it criticism? Or is it that other convenient abdication from standards of performance and judgment practiced by so many artists and critics that they, like certain writers who deal only in sickness and depravity, "reflect the chaos about them"? Again, whose chaos? Whose depravity?

I had always thought that the prime function of art was to create order *out* of chaos—again, not the order of neatness or rigidity or convention or artifice, but the order of clarity by which one will and one vision could draw the essential truth out of apparent confusion. I still do. It is not enough to use parts of a car to convey the brutality of the machine. This is as slavishly representative, and just as easy, as arranging dried flowers under glass to convey nature.

Speaking of which, i.e., the use of real materials (burlap, old gloves, bottletops) in lieu of pigment, this is what one critic had to say about an exhibition of Assemblage at the Museum of Modern Art last year:

"Spotted throughout the show are indisputable works of art, accounting for a quarter or even a half of the total display. But the remainder are works of non-art, anti-art, and art substitutes that are the aesthetic counterparts of the social deficiencies that land people in the clink on charges of vagrancy. These aesthetic bankrupts . . . have no legitimate ideological roof over their heads and not the price of a square intellectual meal, much less a spiritual sandwich, in their pockets."

But Will It Sell?

I quote these words of John Canaday of *The New York Times* as an example of the kind of criticism which puts responsibility to an intelligent public above popularity with an intellectual coterie. Canaday has the courage to say what he thinks and the capacity to say it clearly: two qualities notably absent from his profession.

Next to art, I would say that appreciation and evaluation in the field of music is the most difficult. For it is rarely possible to judge a new composition at one hearing only. What seems confusing or fragmented at first might well become clear and organic a third time. Or it might not. The only salvation here for the listener is, again, an instinct born of experience and association which allows him to separate intent from accident, design from experimentation, and pretense from conviction. Much of contemporary music is, like its sister art, merely a reflection of the composer's own fragmentation: an absorption in self and symbols at the expense of communication with others. The artist, in short, says to the public: If you don't understand this, it's because you're dumb. I maintain that you are not. You may have to go part way or even halfway to meet the artist, but if you must go the whole way, it's his fault, not yours. Hold fast to that. And remember it too when you read new poetry, that estranged sister of music.

"A multitude of causes, unknown to former times, are now acting with a combined force to blunt the discriminating powers of the mind, and, unfitting it for all voluntary exertion, to reduce it to a state of almost savage torpor. The most effective of these causes are the great national events which are daily taking place and the increasing accumulation of men in cities, where the uniformity of their occupations produces a craving for extraordinary incident, which the rapid communication of intelligence hourly gratifies. To this tendency of life and manners, the literature and theatrical exhibitions of the country have conformed themselves."

This startlingly applicable comment was written in the year 1800 by William Wordsworth in the preface to his "Lyrical

The Culture Bit

Ballads"; and it has been cited by Edwin Muir in his recently published book "The Estate of Poetry." Muir states that poetry's effective range and influence have diminished alarmingly in the modern world. He believes in the inherent and indestructible qualities of the human mind and the great and permanent objects that act upon it, and suggests that the audience will increase when "poetry loses what obscurity is left in it by attempting greater themes, for great themes have to be stated clearly." If you keep that firmly in mind and resist, in Muir's words, "the vast dissemination of secondary objects that isolate us from the natural world," you have gone a long way toward equipping yourself for the examination of any work of art.

When you come to theatre, in this extremely hasty tour of the arts, you can approach it on two different levels. You can bring to it anticipation and innocence, giving yourself up, as it were, to the life on the stage and reacting to it emotionally, if the play is good, or listlessly, if the play is boring; a part of the audience organism that expresses its favor by silence or laughter and its disfavor by coughing and rustling. Or you can bring to it certain critical faculties that may heighten, rather than diminish, your enjoyment.

You can ask yourselves whether the actors are truly in their parts or merely projecting themselves; whether the scenery helps or hurts the mood; whether the playwright is honest with himself, his characters, and you. Somewhere along the line you can learn to distinguish between the true creative act and the false arbitrary gesture; between fresh observation and stale cliché; between the avant-garde play that is pretentious drivel and the avant-garde play that finds new ways to say old truths.

Purpose and craftsmanship—end and means—these are the keys to your judgment in all the arts. What is this painter trying to say when he slashes a broad band of black across a white canvas and lets the edges dribble down? Is it a statement of violence? Is it a self-portrait? If it is *one* of these, has he made you believe it? Or is this a gesture of the ego or a form of therapy? If it shocks you, what does it shock you into?

185

But Will It Sell?

And what of this tight little painting of bright flowers in a vase? Is the painter saying anything new about flowers? Is it different from a million other canvases of flowers? Has it any life, any meaning, beyond its statement? Is there any pleasure in its forms or texture? The question is not whether a thing is abstract or representational, whether it is "modern" or conventional. The question, inexorably, is whether it is good. And this is a decision which only you, on the basis of instinct, experience, and association, can make for yourself. It takes independence and courage. It involves, moreover, the risk of wrong decision and the humility, after the passage of time, of recognizing it as such. As we grow and change and learn, our attitudes can change too, and what we once thought obscure or "difficult" can later emerge as coherent and illuminating. Entrenched prejudices, obdurate opinions are as sterile as no opinions at all.

Yet standards there are, timeless as the universe itself. And when you have committed yourself to them, you have acquired a passport to that elusive but immutable realm of truth. Keep it with you in the forests of bewilderment. And never be afraid to speak up.

HOW COMMON IS VULGARITY?

IT WAS VERY SAD about Mlle. Fleuri. As a member of Charm Corps sent by the Common Market Countries to raise the standard of living in the United States, she had the poor judgment to jot down notes on the back of a Four Seasons' menu, which was subsequently found by a bus boy and widely distributed.

"I am very glad to be among these friendly people," she wrote, "but I was never prepared for the kind of vulgarity you find here in the streets and homes. It is truly distressing to see girls of good families chewing gum and rich suburban ladies appearing in public with their hair on rollers. And the language of the children! There appears to be no refinement of behavior here commensurate with the possession of money and comforts."

An outraged public demanded Mlle. Fleuri's immediate ouster and she went back to Neuchatel in tears. What Americans found particularly intolerable in her comments were the two words "vulgarity" and "refinement"; and if Mlle. Fleuri had been better briefed, she would have known that both words implied standards of judgment incompatible with a democratic society since they reek of distinction, of effeteness, and of class above class. They have, in fact, become slightly archaic.

The latest edition of the Merriam-Webster unabridged dictionary weighs over thirteen pounds, physical proof of the hundred thousand words that have been added to our language in the last quarter century. There is a great deal of talk these days of how the language grows and changes and enriches itself: we now see formally listed and defined expressions which most of us never used ten years ago, or even five. But there is little talk about the words we have dropped simply because they have ceased to be relevant to life today. I can think of a number—beauty, hero, nobility, sacrifice are some—which have come to be an embarrassment to their users: they seem not only trite but mawkish.

Yet I was introduced to Mlle. Fleuri's unfortunate words in my youth by people who not only knew what they meant when they said them, but left me with a clear understanding of their weight and application. A "refined" face, or "refined" features were those so purified and clarified by intellect, discipline, dedication, and ardor that the structure of the "spirit" (arch.) shone through. Refinement was a kind of carriage, a way of moving and dressing, a use of voice and hands, that proclaimed the superior being—superior in perception and attainment rather than in position.

Vulgarity, of course, was quite the opposite: it had to do with coarseness and opacity, both physical and spiritual, with animalistic behavior, with crudeness and the absence or abuse of those faculties which elevate man beyond other beings. To be vulgar was to be offensive to all but the vulgar. And the vulgar were, of course, the common people.

It is unthinkable now to say "the common people," unless one is willing to accept the unthinkable epithet of "snob" and to be relegated to the attic of dead concepts. Even "common," in juxtaposition to people, has become offensive, and those who court popularity in any field can no longer afford the once-acceptable phrase, "the common man."

Yet I believe the word "vulgar" to be valid and contemporary as an adjective, an epithet, and a criticism; and I commend Mlle. Fleuri's use of it to describe the many forms of boorishness and coarseness which are accepted precisely because they are common, and which diminish, by erosion or distortion, the stature of man himself.

One of the main reasons why we have not dared use this word is a composite of enlightenment and evasion. We dare not criticize the vulgarity or animalism of underprivileged groups in our own society, for we are responsible in large part for the ignorance and deprivation which produced them. If slum dwellers throw garbage out of their windows and their children scream obscenities in the street, we blame their condition, not themselves. If youths roam like beasts, raping and marauding, we point to our own sins first. We have, in fact, so entwined cause and effect that when some are brave enough to describe honestly what they see with their own eyes, whether it is Dr. Conant and his slum schools or Miss Michelmore, of the Peace Corps, who wrote uncomplimentary remarks about Nigerian life on a postcard, they are accused automatically of prejudice, of assuming racial and social superiority. The evidence of fact is perpetually obscured by the excuse of cause.

But what of those who enjoy the freedoms and privileges of civilization, who are neither poor, oppressed, nor ignorant? We have here the paradox of democracy and affluence: the frequent combination of a high standard of living with a low standard of behavior. It is the price of freedom without form, for the very fluidity which imposes no limits on men's aspirations also imposes no restraints on his indulgences. A man in a stiff collar must hold his head high; a man in a sport shirt can slouch.

I think the analogy holds true in language as well. The disciplines of grammar and precision of vocabulary force clarity and refinement of thought, where faulty or sloppy usage encourage loose thinking. Tabloid editorials, in which a head of state is called a "bum" and people of divergent opinions are called "pinkos" or "punks" are familiar cases of vulgarization. This is, indeed, the core of demagoguery and rabble-rousing: to appeal to the lowest instincts of men by reducing words to their lowest, most "popular" level. In a wholly cynical assumption of equality through a common language, it is in reality a conscious "talking down"; and it represents vulgarity triumphant over restraint, intellect, and care.

These barbarisms are not confined, however, to tabloids or the sex press. They flourish in the talk of middle and upper-class adolescents and adults, who find it hard to communicate without obscenity; in the beat jargon of far-out jazz buffs and disk jockeys; in the sick greeting cards that sell by the millions; and in the loud, abusive voices of women wearing autumn-haze mink. It is loose talk and ugly talk: a language degraded by mental laziness and the same negligence and lack of deference which allows men to wear beach shirts, and women shorts, in the streets and public places of capital cities.

We have come, in fact, to link refinement with artifice and vulgarity with realism, or honesty. In the critical world, plays and novels concerned with the educated and well-bred rich are automatically suspect, particularly if they are articulate and firmly constructed. Conversely, themes based on the underprivileged and inarticulate, on the primitive, gross, and violent are given prior consideration as being truer to life and showing evidence of creative vigor. Nothing so damns a novelist or playwright as the charge that he has "upper-class" attitudes or an inclination towards the aristocratic tradition. In theatre, in fact, the phrase "drawing-room comedy" is in itself a criticism: nothing important happens in a living room; life is in basements, pads, or back alleys.

In painting too, for a long time now, the accepted cliché of creative vigor has been coarseness and violence: the thick, crusted, overlaid pigment and the heavy, crude stroke. The primitivism here lies not only in orgiastic self-expression but in the application of pigment itself, or a combination of substances —rope, wood, metal, sacking, paper—of abrasive texture.

It is not enough to say that this primitivism was the natural and necessary reaction to the pretty and pretentious academism that preceded it. It has become rather the conscious crudeness that marks, in manners and in mind, the popular fashion.

Add Rock 'n' Roll and the Twist and you fill in a picture of man's blithe retrogression, not to childhood but to ape. Yet this may be a gratuitous insult to primates: an exhibition some time ago of paintings by a Cincinnati chimpanzee called Beauty showed a refinement of taste and expression not always evident at the Guggenheim Museum.

The vulgarization of sex is too well known to require definition. Society is deluged by its physical manifestations, of which the strip tease, girlie magazines, and movie ads are only a few of the elements which reduce sex to a matter of measurements and calisthenics (fast, fast relief) and diminish, through contempt of all but her flesh, the image not only of women but also of love. Between this diminution and vulgarization of the female and the rise of the male homosexual, the tie is plain.

Plain too is the connection between this daily exposure to sex and the precocity of our children, specially the ways in which they are forced into adult patterns of dress and speech and play.

The Culture Bit

The six-year-old boy in long pants and a snap-brim hat and the little girl he "dates" with permanented hair and fingernail polish are victims of this process, which begins by destroying their visual innocence and ends by destroying the best of childhood while it keeps them from growing up. Underneath the love talk and the TV-serial wise-guy patter are the arrested kids, playing sex and marriage before they know of love.

At the other end of this process are the older women who dress and act like teen-agers and the older men who wear strange hats at conventions and tell dirty jokes. The perversion of age into false youth produces such familiar vulgarities as the old leg in knee-length skirts and the old face under layers of make-up and baby blonde hair. All these phenomena Mlle. Fleuri might have jotted on her menu, together with such inanimate manifestations of the synthetic as iron pelicans on lawns and plastic Christs above steering wheels. The primitive can be, and often is, beautiful. The vulgar is invariably ugly.

But Mlle. Fleuri should really have stayed around until Christmas. The little plaster image in cars is only a small part of that obfuscation of His meaning which we have come to take for granted every year. The frenetic orgy of buying, with its attendant harassment of body and soul, may boost the economy and gladden acquisitive hearts of young and old, but if Christ is the ultimate refinement of man, then this is the ultimate vulgarity. Yet we excuse it in the name of the prosperity which created it and which imposes no limit on material craving.

It can be argued that all these indulgences, whether distorting the face by chewing gum or distorting the language by abusing words, are unimportant, particularly if the indulgers have good hearts. And yet the degree of a culture is marked not by possessions or comforts so much as by behavior; and refinement—of senses, of manners, of feeling, and of expression—might be a very valid national goal for a wealthy democracy. It is in any case the price of privilege.

Come back, Mlle. Fleuri!

THE CONFESSION OF MARK GUTZLER

TO: THE UNITED STATES ADVISORY
BOARD FOR LITERARY EXCELLENCE

After the public chastisement so rightly administered to me
by USABLE, I feel it imperative to make a full and open apology
to your distinguished body and to the American people for any
and all unwitting deviations I have made from the true direction
of American writing as established with such brilliance and
foresight by the independent coterie of scholars, critics, writers,
and publishers who decide what is good and what is bad in this
country.

With a heavy heart and a cleansed spirit, I accept the new
critical standards of the day and confess to the following sins
against literary worth as defined by USABLE.

The first sin was committed not by me but by my parents,
who failed to belong to an oppressed minority, who lived in
middle-class comfort in an urban section without literary value,
being neither in slum nor in ghetto, and neither in the South
nor in the Middle West, and who held each other in mutual
respect as long as they lived. It has been a source of continuing
anguish to me as a writer that their kind of life, if indeed it can
be called such, produced none of the festering hatreds which
alone give experience and, to the written account of experience,
validity. USABLE has rightly accused me of fostering a personality
cult: that is, of giving the impression in my writings that some
persons are good, or noble. I know now that this is not so and

that we are all equally vile. My parents were vile in denying this.

They were responsible also, unfortunately, for the fact that my adolescence was neither particularly painful nor confused, and therefore not worth chronicling. I had, of course, trouble with my skin and the usual stirrings of sex, but I remember being very happy fishing alone, mountain climbing, and cataloguing rock specimens. I also played the flute, an offensively pure instrument. None of this, I now see, is suitable background for a serious writer.

I further confess with shame to a long apprenticeship in the art and craft of writing. That this is a weakening and perverting experience I now, to my sorrow, admit. To quote USABLE's indictment: "Knowledge of the structure and use of language can produce a graceful style wholly incongruous to the realities of the present and, what is worse, can give the reader a simple pleasure incompatible with the recognition of true art." I was led astray in my youth by the sinful love of words and a slavish attention to the so-called masters of literature of the past. My writing has therefore been progressively sapped of the qualities of accident and error that give strength and importance to the best of contemporary writing. In a misguided attempt, moreover, to perfect the skill of communicating clearly to others, I have sacrificed that priceless ingredient of true talent: obscurity. As USABLE stated, clarity bears the stigma of order, and order is the enemy of the natural state of man, chaos. The true writer reflects chaos.

The reviewers of my verse—who, of course, were members of USABLE—brought this out some time ago in criticizing what one of them described as "the triviality of the explicit," complaining that the use of rhyme, meter, and humor automatically removed it from important consideration. Again, it was felt that the public was seduced (hence cheated) by the ease of reading and understanding. At the time, I felt this judgment was unjust; now I know it to be painfully correct. In the future I will make comprehension as difficult as possible in the hopes of being praised by the critics if not read by the public. I fear I have favored the latter at the expense of the former.

I confess further to a grievous sin of omission: lack of symbolism. My writing, except in rare instances of innocent accident, has been on one level instead of two. This is because I have kept shamefully aloof from other writers whose symbols I could share, thus exiling myself from that intergroup dialogue which USABLE rightly calls the Literary Core. I admit also to not knowing enough symbols, possibly the result of intellectual impoverishment through ignorance of faculty conversations and academic reviews.

Of all USABLE's charges against me, perhaps the most serious is the use of restraint and moderation. I now realize that the damning presence of these inhibitors in my work is the result of cowardice and, worse, of taste. A thorough examination of my collected writings revealed only six four-letter words and two consummations of the sex act, and concerning the latter, the examiners noted grave ommissions of detail that were subsequently filed under the heading "Evasion of Reality." Under this same heading I have been accused of failing to deal with incest, perversion, addiction, prostitution, and rape. It is to my eternal regret that my life circumstances did not happen to involve me directly with any of these acts and conditions. My pitifully meager lot was to have been educated in sex by a pleasant older woman and to have been married to the same wife for fifteen years. In my own defense, however, I must state categorically that I am very fond of liquor and have been known to pass out on various occasions, one of them particularly disgusting.

In general, the omission of repulsive or clinically sexual detail in my works has been due to a belief—mistaken, I now know— that something should be left to the imagination of the reader. USABLE's strictures have made me realize that this is in fact a

The Culture Bit

public disservice, since what the reader imagines is worse than any reality and therefore potentially more damaging, psychologically and emotionally, than the printed word.

USABLE accuses me of deliberately avoiding the revived form of fiction called picaresque, in which wild or wildly comic episodes succeed each other for five or six hundred pages with no discernible point except the exuberance of the author. My failure to be picaresque is not intentional. Rather, I fear, it is a combination of chronic lassitude and, once more, that sterile compulsion toward form and organization which has, more than anything, caused me such public humiliation at the hands of my critics.

It may interest USABLE to learn, however, that my next book will concern the adventures of two midgets, one fund raiser, three dictators, and fourteen whores working in an imaginary Alliance for Progress. I have no idea how it will come out.

Against USABLE's final charge—that, since no writer more than forty years old can presume to be hailed as a "talent," I have no literary future—I can muster no defense. It is quite understandable that important critics concern themselves more with promise than performance, since praise of the former is less onerous than judgment of the latter. My new book, *Naked Belch*, promises to be very promising.

In conclusion, I wish to thank the United States Advisory Board for Literary Excellence for showing me my grievous errors and lighting a new path toward creative value. I am a new man, and a new writer.

Humbly yours,
MARK GUTZLER
(Formerly know as
Marya Mannes)

6: *The Carriers*

PREFACE
WHAT'S WRONG WITH OUR PRESS?
THE LOST TRIBE OF TELEVISION
MASSIVE DETERGENCE

PREFACE

SO MUCH HAS BEEN SAID about mass
communications in the last two decades that I have chosen to
spare the reader most of my own written or spoken observations
over a ten-year period, offering only those few which seem, to me
at least, to contain some special insights. These concern the
archaism of most of the nation's press; the divorce of the intellectual from television (and what it has done to both); and, less
importantly but still worth noting, the phenomenon of the daytime serial.

Beyond that, the tenor of my thinking has led to two conclusions. One is that the more people are reached by mass communications, the less they communicate with each other. The proliferation of one-way messages, whether in print or on air, seems to
have increased rather than lessened the alienation of the individual. Friendly, gregarious America is full of intensely lonely

people for whom radio and television provide the illusory solace of company.

The second conclusion is closely related to the first: namely, that the more mass communications are a business, dependent on and inextricably joined with mass selling, the more questionable is the value of their service in over-all human terms. The familiar counterargument is that many of the cultural and informational contributions now available to millions on television and radio would never reach them without advertising support. If this is so, it is all the more to be questioned whether anything so important as the enlightenment of a people should depend on private profits or remain solely in private hands. The British Broadcasting Company, free from either government or commercial control and probably the finest mass communication service in the world, is an eloquent No. A system such as ours, based on delivering (the word is significant) the largest possible audience to a sponsor at the lowest possible cost per thousand, may increase revenue, but it diminishes human worth. No man should be a fraction of a point in a Nielsen rating.

I am fully aware of the enormous costs of television and the infinitely complex problem of paying for them. But I am equally aware of human ingenuity unfettered by special interests and past precedents. There are, there will be, other ways of paying for television than program sponsorship; and in earlier pages of this book I have mentioned such alternative noncommercial services as the educational network and listener-foundation-supported radio to provide the public with the real company of ideas and illuminations rather than the shadow solace of mass entertainment.

As for commercial television itself, it is so deeply entrenched in its present and profitable pattern that it would never of its own volition bring about the substantive changes that the public interest (if not the public will) demands. One such change would be sharp limitation of the length and frequency of commercials, another would quarantine them in specific blocs—like sales catalogues of the air—between, but never during, programs; thus freeing the viewer from the gross harassment and indignity of interruption while he looks at a play or a documentary or a movie of any length.

Ultimately, the measure of performance in any mass media is the degree of obligation assumed towards the people it serves. The greatest achievements of commercial TV have been those prompted by decisions to give viewers what an awareness of their needs as intelligent citizens dictated they should see; regardless of cost, of pressures, or of the chance of failure. Anyone who has ever worked in a network knows how rarely such decisions triumph over the ratings and agency pressures.

When they do, they deserve the strongest public support. This is where you, and the intellectual abstainers dealt with later come in.

WHAT'S WRONG WITH OUR PRESS?

NOTE: In 1960, the Women's National Press Club invited two speakers to address the Association of Newspaper Editors. One was Mrs. Clare Boothe Luce, the other Mrs. Eleanor Roosevelt, and each was to speak for twenty minutes on the subject "What's Wrong with Our Press?"

Shortly before the event, Mrs. Roosevelt suffered a minor accident, and I was asked to substitute for her.

It is, I think, pertinent to remark here that although this speech had wide repercussions in Washington and across the country, only

But Will It Sell?

the Woman's Page of *The Washington Post* featured it prominently and no single newspaper printed it in full or in substantial part. *Time,* understandably, omitted it entirely, and of the news magazines only *The Reporter,* to which I was attached, published a slightly condensed text.

NEWSPAPERS have two great advantages over television. They can be used by men as barriers against their wives. It is still the only effective screen against the morning features of the loved one, and, as such, performs a unique human service. The second advantage is that you can't line a garbage pail with a television set—it's usually the other way around.

But here are some interesting statistics from a little, and little known, survey by Mr. Roper called "The Public's Reaction to Television Following the Quiz Investigations." In it he asks everybody but me this question: Suppose you could continue to have only one of the following—radio, television, newspapers, or magazines—which would you prefer? Newspapers came in second: Forty-two per cent said if they could only have one, they would keep television. Thirty-two per cent said if they could only have one, they would keep newspapers.

Even so, newspaper people should be much happier than the magazine people, because only four per cent said they needed magazines, as against nineteen per cent for radio.

But listen to this. Mr. Roper asked these same harried people: "If you get conflicting or different reports of the same news story from radio, television, the magazines, and the newspapers, which of the four versions would you be most inclined to believe?" Thirty-two per cent believe newspapers as against thirty per cent who believe television. But then something really strange happens. When Mr. Roper asked his guinea pigs *which* of these media they would be *least* inclined to believe, the newspapers topped the list. In a big way, too. Twenty-four per cent don't believe newspapers as against nine per cent who don't believe television. And though I'm as leery of certain polls as anyone, this margin of credulity is too wide to be discounted.

The Carriers

The fact is that although network television still allots too little time to the vital service of informing the public, it does a better job in that little time than the nation's press as a whole. And when I speak of the nation's press as a whole, I am *not* speaking of the five or six splendid newspapers—and the one great newspaper—which serve the world as models of responsible public information. I am speaking of the local press which in hundreds of American communities is the *only* news available, aside from those recitals of ticker tape that pass for radio news, and which defaults on its obligations to the public.

Why do I think network TV does a better job of informing than these papers? Well, let's get the partisan bit over with. Television lives on advertising to an even greater extent than newspapers, and since advertising is big business, advertising is by nature Republican. Yet nowhere in network newscasts or network commentaries on current events have I encountered the intense partisanship, the often rabid bias that colors the editorial pages of the majority of newspapers in this country. Douglass Cater, in his book *The Fourth Branch of Government*, confines himself to only one pungent footnote on this subject. "I have deliberately avoided," he writes, "getting into the predominantly one-party nature of newspaper ownership. It is a fact of life." This particular fact of life is a shameful one: that newspapers whose duty it is to inform the American public give them only one side of the issues that affect them profoundly—the Republican side. This is shameful not only for Democrats—they have survived it before and will survive it again—but for the maturity of our people. Some of the same papers which loudly extol the virtues of free enterprise and a free press are consistently failing to print the facts on which a people can form a balanced and independent opinion. That balanced and independent opinion is our only real security as a nation.

Now, very often, television coverage of news is superficial and inadequate. Very often the picture takes precedence over the point. But by and large the news reports and commentaries on CBS and NBC and ABC make every effort to present viewers with more than one aspect of an issue, either by letting opposing spokesmen have their say, or by outlining the positions held by both major parties on the subject involved.

Television also provides a wide range of opinion by setting up four or five experts and letting them knock each other down. What has the local press of this nature? Is it discharging its duty to diversity by printing snippets of opinion from unqualified readers? Is this exploring an issue?

Television may not have a Lippmann or a Reston, but then, what papers in America can claim an Eric Sevareid, a Walter Cronkite, a Huntley or a Brinkley, or—although he is invisible—an Edward Morgan?

Another thing. Among the leading commentators on television, you find no Pegler, no Winchell, no Fulton Lewis Jr. Fortunately for the American public, television does not tolerate the kind of distortion of fact, the kind of partisan virulence and personal peeve, that many newspapers not only welcome but encourage. In its entertainment, television caters far too much to the lowest instincts of man, particularly the lust for violence and—at the opposite end of the spectrum—the urge to escape from reality into sedation. But there is one appetite it does not feed and which the partisan newspapers of the nation do: the appetite for hate—hate of whatever is different. I do not find on television the kind of editorials chronic in the New York tabloids as well as in many local papers across the country where the techniques of demagoguery prevail: Rouse the Rabble by Routing Reason.

A newspaper has the right—the duty even—to assume an attitude, to take a position. But it has an equally sacred right to explain that position in the light of the opposing one, to document that position, and to bolster it, not with emotion but with fact.

Here, of course, is where background information helps the public to draw its conclusions. TV does a great deal of this in the form of documentaries, and you can of course say that they have the time and the money to do this and you haven't. Yet across this wide country, and with the exception of a handful of syndicated columns, I fail to find in any local paper any attempt, however minimal, to strengthen this muscle of digestion, without which news can neither nourish nor inform. It can only stuff. Between the opinions of the editor and the bare statements of the wire services there is nothing, nothing, that is, except a collection of snippets used as fillers between the ads and picked at random.

One of the greatest and most justified criticisms of television has been that in appealing to the largest audience possible, it neglects minority audiences and minority tastes. This is still largely true. But there is, perhaps, one program a day and many, of course, on Sunday which an intelligent man or woman can enjoy and derive interest from. In my trips east or west or north or south, I pick up the local paper to find this enjoyment or interest—in vain. Now, surely there's something wrong here. Many of these places I've visited—and I'm sure this is true of the whole country—have college communities where highly intelligent and talented people live, whether they are teachers or doctors or lawyers or musicians or scientists. What is there for them in the paper, usually the only paper, of their town? What features are provided for these people? What stimulation? How many times have I heard them say: "If you want to see what a really bad paper is like, read our sheet." When a local paper has a monopoly in a region, as most of them do, why is it necessary to aim at the lowest common denominator?

I believe that over a period of decades newspapers have become a habit rather than a function. They have held their franchise so long that change has become inadmissible. I do not know, in fact, of any medium that has changed as little in the last twenty years as the daily press. And this resistance to change is the end of growth—which, in turn, marks the end of usefulness.

Change means trouble, change means work, change means cost. It is easier to print wire services dispatches than have a reporter on the beat. It is easier to buy syndicated columns

than find—and train—local talent. It is easier to let the ads
dictate the format than develop a format that elevates news
above dogfood. It is easier to write editorial copy that appeals
to emotion rather than reason. And in handling straight news,
it is easier to assume the pious mantle of objectivity than to
edit. To quote Eric Sevareid: "Our rigid formulae of so-called
objectivity, beginning with the wire agency bulletins and reports—the warp and woof of what the papers print . . . our flat,
one-dimensional handling of news, have given the lie the same
prominence and impact that truth is given. They have elevated
the influence of fools to that of wise men; the ignorant to the
level of the learned; the evil to the level of the good." This
featureless objectivity is nothing less than the editor's abdication of responsibility and is just as dangerous as the long and
subtle processing of fact to fit a policy that characterizes certain
weekly magazines. The one is dereliction; the other is deception. And both may provide a reason for the decline of public
confidence in their press.

This is, to me, a tragedy. I am a printed-word woman myself,
and I still think the word was not only in the beginning but will
be in the end. No picture can ever be an adequate substitute.
The word will prevail; that is, if you, who are its guardians, treat
it with the respect it deserves. For if you degrade and cheapen
the word too long, the people will turn to the picture. They are
beginning to turn to the picture now. Not in New York, maybe,
not in Washington, D.C., or St. Louis, or two or three other
cities, but in hundreds of towns across the country. Oh, they will
buy your papers—to hold up at breakfast or to line the trash can
or to light a fire. But not to learn. And you may wake up one
day to find you have lost the greatest power entrusted to men: to
inform a free people.

THE LOST TRIBE OF TELEVISION

YOU'VE HEARD THEM, maybe you're one of them: the people who say, "Oh, I never look, I wouldn't have a set in the house." Or "No, we don't own one. There just isn't time to look." Or, simply, "It's all so lousy, there's nothing worth looking at."

Who are they? Well, a few might reside in the Social Register, where any mass medium is vulgar and where television is something the cook keeps in her room. A few might live in remote parts of the nation where mountains intercept the image or where men prefer nature to artifice. But most of the people who find television beneath their notice are intellectuals.

What really is an intellectual? Businessmen—and that would describe most broadcasters and advertisers—would like to think him a desiccated Brain buried in books, with a preference for plain wives, dull food, and abstract talk. Certainly his kind—both male and female—exist, speaking an impenetrable critical jargon of their own, looking for symbols instead of sense, living aloof from the sweat and clamor of simple men. They are, as one intellectual has said, "educated beyond their intelligence."

But the dictionary has a broader definition, describing intellect as "the ability to reason, perceive, or understand," and as "high intelligence." And I have an even broader one. I would call an intellectual one whose instrument of work—his mind—is also his major source of pleasure; a man whose entertainment is his intelligence. Because of his inner resources, his knowledge, his curiosity, and the disciplines of his training, he can divert himself by his own thoughts and perceptions, bringing to books, music, science, and art as much as he takes out of them. Since he provides his own company, the productive intellectual is seldom bored with solitude or silence. And when he seeks the company of others, it is—through talk—for the further play of thought. This is the man who will say, "I have no time for television; my life is full." Or he will say, "Oh, sometimes I turn on wrestling or the late-late show," as one would say "sometimes I take a pill when I can't sleep." And if this intellectual owns a television set, he will use it—if ever—as he would a mystery paperback, for sedative purposes. What is more likely, though, is that he doesn't own one at all. Not because he can't afford the money but because he can't afford the time. And because he has turned the knob idly at the house of friends or in some hotel and been aghast at what he has seen, he will tell you, with complete authority, that "television stinks." Like a man surveying a newsstand and saying "print stinks," he is partially right. But where he is quick to associate himself with the best in print, whether it be *The New York Times, Harper's, The Reporter,* or the *Bulletin of Atomic Scientists,* he is totally ignorant of the best in television. And where his voice is raised in support of creative efforts in little reviews which very few read, it is silent here—through ignorance of that area of excellence in television, however small, which millions of Americans see. By and large, the intellectual has detached himself from TV right from the start, and in so doing he has not only impoverished his American culture by depriving the greatest medium of mass communication of his own talents, but he has also cut himself off from the mainstream. This is an abdication of responsibility at his own peril.

For if the intellectual turns away from television, he turns away from the vast majority of his countrymen, to whom he can no longer speak in mutually recognizable terms. I am reminded here of a brilliant writer-editor who returned to this country after some time abroad to edit one of our most distinguished journals of fact and opinion. After one brief look at television, he refused to buy a set, nor would he read any TV ads in the newspapers or magazines.

"Why should I clutter up my head with that stuff?" he said.

I was tempted to answer that if he didn't, he had no right to address himself to the American people: he was ignoring the enveloping fabric of our society.

I would now openly make the same charge against many others.

What right has a minister to address his congregation when he has no concept of the moral values, or lack of values, it derives from television hours of every day? What right has the teacher to instruct pupils when he doesn't know what they are being taught on their home screens every day of every week? How can anyone presume to nourish, instruct, or elevate the American mind when he has no familiarity with its daily diet— or, for that matter, any part in composing its substance? It is perfectly true that the businessmen of television have been extremely slow to press those of superior intelligence into the medium's service, but it is equally true that intellectuals have been very reluctant to proffer themselves, either as critics or creators. Simply by abstention they have denied their talents and superior intelligence to an undernourished public. Isn't the crux of the matter really that television is of so little use to the intellectual because he has been of so little use to it?

We can blame this, I think, on the dangerous divorce between science and the humanities which has ranged the technician and the scientist on one side, and the scholar and the artist on the other, when in fact they are both limbs of the same creative organism. There was no connection between the men who invented the cathode tube and the men who could give it speech and purpose; and the intellectual failed to realize, as he should have from the start, that television could be to modern man what the printing press was to medieval man: the most powerful means of spreading knowledge and ideas so far discovered. In-

But Will It Sell?

stead, the intellectual watched his precocious child in the same way as he had watched the beginnings of radio—with distaste and skepticism—and turned away, shrugging. And then, of course, as with radio, the hucksters took over. Overnight, the miracle was sold—down the river—to the highest bidders, and the public air became, in fact, private profit.

If, fourteen years ago, men of high intelligence had said: "Before this medium becomes public we must determine exactly what it is, what its functions and duties are, and where it is going"; if a national commission composed of these men and women had been formed to draw up a charter for television; if the best minds in the country had had the vision to think in the great terms which a great medium deserved, we might not now be in the midst of a season in which evening television watchers are able to see forty-six crime and violence plus western programs and twenty-three situation comedies each week, in which eighty per cent of the total programming is dead film or tape instead of live reality, and in which sixty million Americans are being sold instead of being told a third of their day. Intellectuals would nod a solemn agreement to Dr. Charles Siepmann of New York University who, before a hearing of the Federal Communications Commission, said: "I don't believe private enterprise is good for Americans in the degree to which it involves the pursuit of profit without end at the price of intelligence and virtue."

But nodding and deploring are not enough. Nor is it enough for intellectuals to give their services and talents, as a number are now doing, to nonprofit educational television. NET (The National Educational Television and Radio Center) is making great strides in spite of continuing shortage of money and shortage of outlets; and a limited number of Americans can now see fine plays, concerts, ballets, films, and instructional programs without commercial interruptions on about 70 stations across the country. But when you compare this with 449 commercial stations, you realize what a stepchild of communications NET still is.

The Carriers

Now the intellectuals who detach themselves from television say, "There you are again. Commercial television is by its very nature dependent on a mass audience. It is a consumer-based medium. The minority that might want what we have to give is presumably not worth programming for, and what we have to say isn't for the mass anyway."

The audience ratings on some of commercial television's high-level fare would support their argument. But the refutations are growing. The mass was fascinated by Maugham's "The Moon and Sixpence" when it was superbly produced by David Susskind and acted by Sir Laurence Olivier. The mass was profoundly impressed by the CBS Report, "Population Explosion," a brilliant exploration of the very touchy subject of birth control or, more accurately, of its absence in India. The mass tunes in faithfully to a news team of two men, Chet Huntley and David Brinkley, who daily bring perception, wisdom, and wit to their chronicle of the world's events. The mass, it is reported, has even stayed with Walter Lippmann through his annual hours of television talk with Howard K. Smith. And it is symptomatic of television's estate and the intellectual's abstention from it that it took years, and the caliber of a Howard K. Smith, to persuade Mr. Lippmann to expose himself on the air. Writing of this program, John Crosby of the *New York Herald Tribune* said: "I have felt most urgently that television should more often use its unique powers to bring us the great leaders and thinkers of our time, to inspire and lift and to shape our thinking and our personalities."

True. But how many great thinkers think in terms of television, of communicating directly with millions? How many speak a common language?

"All right," says the intellectual, "but what is this common language, and how do I learn to speak it: by wasting my time looking at hours of dribble and nonsense on a small screen when I'd rather be reading a book or listening to music or talking with friends?"

The first thing I'd tell him would be: find out what good

But Will It Sell?

television is. Read the best critics of television regularly: the men and women who know the best and the worst, who apply discriminating standards to what they see, who are familiar with the actual workings of the medium. Read the listings in the daily paper where the outstanding programs are described for convenience and choose one that, because of the individuals involved or the subject treated, promises interest. On Sunday you will have plenty to choose from, in a range from discussion to drama, from documentary to song. And at least once a week, if you watch for it, some network documentary or live coverage of an actual event should claim your attention. One of the intellectual's pet fallacies is that having a set imposes the duty of looking at it regularly; that it somehow forces unwilling attention. This is, of course, nonsense. Television is an instrument that can be used when wanted. It may not be wanted for six days and nights of the week, but on the seventh it may provide something which no other instrument, no other medium, can provide.

And what, says our intellectual, might that be? Well, it might be confrontation with some world leader, some mover of men, whose face and manner might be more illuminating of his character than all his printed speeches put together. It might be access to some actual event—the four days of terrible tragedy in Dallas and Washington last November were shared, thanks to television, by the entire nation. No other medium could have so involved our millions. It could be a deliberation of the United Nations, where the expressions of delegates and the tone of their voices tell more than words, and where the patterns of hostility or compromise are clearly woven. It might be the flights into space, the tracking of one man on his celestial journey. More than others, the home-bound intellectual lives alone and apart much of the time. The door must be closed on contemplation, the outer world shut out to provide that enclosure so vital to thought. And it can be a boon to him to project himself, by simply turning a knob, into the world of action, of distance, of difference. This is television's major miracle for intellectuals: not

212

to entertain, not to distract, not to relax, but to illuminate by presenting reality.

A minority of television fare? Indeed—and alas—yes. But one of the reasons it *is* a minority is precisely that it receives no support from the people towards whom it is aimed: the people with "the ability to reason, perceive, or understand"; the people of "high intelligence."

Do these people, the intellectuals, know the profound discouragement of a man like Fred Friendly when, after a superlative CBS Report on an issue of great urgency he walks into a roomful of intelligent and sophisticated people not one of whom had bothered to turn it on?

There are brilliant and dedicated men in television who fight against constant odds to bring the truth to the people, to infuse beauty and meaning in their daily fare, to lift television to its great potential. And when, at last, some of their efforts succeed, who listens to them, who acknowledges them, who argues for them? The intellectuals? Hardly ever. They weren't looking. The most articulate voices in the country are the least heard. So the commercial masters of television say, "See? We try to put on high-level stuff, but where's the audience for it? And the agencies decide they're better off with another crime show or another variety.

It is time, then, that intellectuals learned a little humility; at least enough to recognize that a five-minute talk by a man like Ed Morgan or Howard K. Smith or Eric Sevareid might do more to inform the American people than six issues of "little reviews" or a fifty-page thesis; enough to recognize that among this audience there may be more potential intelligence than in the clusters of erudition on the nation's campuses. It is this intelligence that cries for enlightenment, for standards, for direction, which it does not receive from intellectuals who stand aloof.

Senator Mike Monroney of Oklahoma once said, "Perhaps I am more ambitious for this vital means of communication than those who render it their professional services. Its potential is so great as an educational medium, as a cultural stimulant, as a door to all the beautiful and thrilling things of the world. It seems to me its horizons are unlimited." And later he said, "America is made up of people most of whom, in the long run, can appreciate the difference in the effect on the lives of their children between a tour of Yucatan's historic ruins and a tour of the assorted saloons which make up the stage set for Tombstone, Arizona. The difference may not show up in the Neilsen ratings, but it will show up in the classroom grades and ideals of the next generation of Americans."

If the intellectual continues to ignore television, he will pay for it in the end by having to speak to people incapable of understanding him, to teach people distracted by trivia and corrupted by commerce: a people abandoned to the cheapest use of a great medium.

MASSIVE DETERGENCE

THERE ARE TIMES when about five million television viewers get mad simultaneously. It is when the networks assume their obligations to the American public and show them events of importance, whether a man in space or a President in trouble, between noon and five P.M. when their favorite soap operas are normally visible. Then the letters pour in, saying "How dare you?" or "How can you?"

The soap operas, as even those who have never seen them

The Carriers

know, are so called because they are sponsored largely by cleaning products, though prepared foods and other household items
help pick up the tab. There are nine of them, each lasting twelve
to twenty-two minutes. Of the estimated five millions addicted to
one or more Soaps a day, the majority are home-bound women,
augmented by invalids, nightworkers, the unemployed, and the
retired. And although I am not one of them, I know something of
the compulsion that draws them to their sets.

I started looking simply to find out what they were like, for
I felt that anything which claimed the attention of so sizable a
group of Americans warranted my own. I looked at them clinically from time to time, fascinated by the separate world in which
they moved, by their formulas, their characterizations, their tricks,
and, if indeed there is one apart from selling soap, their purpose.
I was held, too, by the over-all excellence of the acting and direction, the ingenuity of the plotting, and a casting little short of
inspired: the performers had become the people.

My clinical interest still remains, but the daytime serials I now
view serve another purpose: brainwashing. I find nothing that
rests a mind better after a few hours of thinking and writing than
a short breather around midday or mid-afternoon, for a Soap
makes no claims whatever on the intelligence. On the contrary, it
suspends it. With music one must think of something. With these
serials one can think of nothing. One floats in a never-never land
perfectly conveyed by titles that mean absolutely nothing: "Love
of Life," "Search for Tomorrow," "Guiding Light," "As the World
Turns," "The Secret Storm," "Edge of Night." But there are no
edges. All is suffused, formless, unresolving, unending. And with
the many small credibilities, the minutiae of reality, all is incredible.

Or is it, I wondered, incredible only to me? Is this the way
most of us think and feel? Would we act as they do in given
circumstances? Do these serials tell us, in oversimplified form,
what kind of people we really are?

There is no question of their wide popular acceptance, confined though it may be to a special and largely feminine segment

of viewers. The volume of letters to CBS and NBC is evidence enough of the involvement they feel in the families they watch on screen: distress over deaths, resentment of "villains," advice on child rearing. Serial actors are constantly accosted on the street by strangers who greet them as old friends, met every weekday for years on end. To the truly addicted, the people in soap operas are important company, a part of their lives.

Who are they? I can speak with authority of the characters in "Search for Tomorrow," "The Guiding Light," "As the World Turns," "The Secret Storm," and "Edge of Night," and they fall quite easily into certain groupings. One is the Mother of the Family, characterized in at least three of these serials by women of a monumental stupidity. It is hard to decide which is the most obtuse: Mrs. Hughes in "As the World Turns," Mrs. Bergman in "Search for Tomorrow," or Mrs. Bauer in "The Guiding Light." These ladies rarely stir out of their kitchens (the counters of which are totally free of food), never open a book, never turn on a record player, and preface every statement, at no matter what hour, with an offer of a cup of coffee. Their provinciality is stupefying: they can talk of nothing but personal matters, many of which are none of their business. They pry into the lives of their children and their neighbors and their friends with no compunction, proffering judgment or advice when it is least required.

MOTHER: "Did you go out with Don last night?"

DAUGHTER: "Yes."

MOTHER: "Did you have a good time? What did you talk about? Has he proposed? Do you think you should go on seeing him if he hasn't?"

And so forth.

Reticence is unheard of. Lives, like suburban lawns, are common property. It is made very clear by the writers that these are the salt of the earth: fine mothers and housewives who know their place in the home. Yet these same women never let go of their children. None of them can bear to see their grown sons leave their house, and if their grown daughters marry they are expected to spend much of their spare time in the parental home, confiding in Mom and Dad. I have yet to hear one serial Mother tell her son to go out and be a man, or advise her daughter to stand on her own feet. Maternal love in a Soap is the degree to which you bind your family to you, and if one of the bonds is loosened, it can be to no good end.

Another category of female is the Difficult Daughter. Ellen in "As the World Turns," Susan in "The Secret Storm," and Penny in "As the World Turns" are prime examples of young women who should have had their bottoms whacked daily since childhood and their aberrations knocked out of them by men, whether father or suitor. Willful, sentimental, inclined to hysteria, and largely foolish, they are yet presumed to be objects of love or pity. Though they make the lives of others intolerable, they are the beneficiaries of tolerance. I remember myself applauding quietly when the suffering parents in "The Secret Storm" could stand their Susan no longer and accused her of being the bitch she was.

I can think of only two girls in these serials who make young American womanhood supportable. One is a teen-ager called Amy, sister of the terrible Susan, who is not only intelligent but educated, direct, and humorous. I suspect that her independence of spirit will crumble at the touch of love, and instead of immersing herself in poetry and drama, she will find True Happiness in the kitchen.

I thought, a while back, that a delightful girl called Janet, in "Search for Tomorrow," might have conducted her life with some sense in spite of retarded parents, but she decided to return to a young lout to whom she was married before she married a nice doctor because she thought the lout was dead, but he wasn't, and she's having a baby by the doctor, to whom she is *not* married but he doesn't know it. If you don't understand that, skip it. It's clear as crystal to me and to 4,999,999 other people.

Nearly every Soap has a Tiresome Grandfather. In "As the World Turns" there is Pa, who slops around his son's house in suspenders and old sweaters emitting little wisdoms of mawkish banality. There is Judge Lowell in the same serial, a television writer's image of the old-school gentleman, all pompous integrity and legal rectitude. And there is Myra Ames's father in "The Secret Storm," personification of another favorite television image, the intellectual. This retired professor lives with his books, quotes copiously from the classics, and is an odious meddler, full of dangerous sophistries. There is lovable old Papa Bauer in "The Guiding Light," who speaks with a heavy German accent and out of his simple wisdom knows the score. He also tells it.

The younger male generation in Soaps is what one might expect: adolescents with callow voices who are preoccupied first with becoming doctors or lawyers and second with dating their neighbor's daughter. If they are not Lovable, they are Problems Who Need Help. The Help is given by the parents who have made them Problems in the first place, or by the Love of the Right Girl. In rare moments of revelation, the boys get impatient with Mom, but in the end they realize they never had it so good as when she sewed on their buttons.

It is encouraging to report, however, that of all these categories the most sympathetic are the Wise Fathers. Dad is a pretty good Joe, and the only thing the matter with Chris Hughes or Peter Ames or Doug Casson is that they don't divorce their wives or at least knock some sense into them. When their irritation with Mom becomes insupportable (and that should be daily, but isn't), they usually leave the room. Only rarely do they lash out at the little woman, and this is hastily followed by a scene of reconciliation in which a tender embrace gives Mom the right to make an ass of herself again in the next installment. The American husband is a chronic martyr.

The matter of professions in Soaps is revealing. If these good men can't be doctors, they are lawyers. Stu Bergman, to be sure, runs a motor haven and sells cars, but then he's a simpler fellow. Arthur Tate runs something called Tate Enterprises, which is never explained, but then what is business but sitting at a desk and saying "Will you come in for a minute?" on the intercom. Detectives and police commissioners are all right, particularly in a serial which, like "Edge of Night," concerns itself largely with crime and the law; and I do remember one engineer. Being president of a department store is fine, and Peter Ames actually does talk of stocks and sales and turnovers. Journalists can get under the wire if they expose vice, but if they just write novels, they're unreliable. If you can be a Man of God, as Richard the minister was in the defunct "The Brighter Day," you are, of course, the greatest.

But watch out for the arts. A prime cad in "The Guiding Light" was a fellow who ran an art gallery. He had all the vices: he was sophisticated, widely traveled, a Connossoor, and considerably older than the girl he wished to wed. Unfortunately, he has since become a Good Guy.

Of occupations for women, only nursing and secretarial work are really justified, and then only to fill the time between romances or after disaster. A Soap woman works Instead, never For; and the mere fact of leaving home during the day is a sign of deep emotional disturbance. Sometimes one of the Difficult Daughters takes a job: the impossible Ellen spent several months running a bookshop to try to forget the illegitimate baby she gave away, but in every sequence someone would tell her that work was bad for her, it was only an escape. No decent serial female wants to be anything but a wife and mother, and the Soaps are full of able-bodied and pretty-faced girls languishing because they are neither instead of having fun in the world. In television it is unthinkable to make use of your brains, possibly because you have none.

The serials are peopled mainly by White Anglo-Saxon Protestants, but once in a while, just to show the melting pot, we have our German Papa Bauer or a young man of Italian origin called Torino (but he was clean-cut), and one or two characters who look vaguely Jewish but have names like Brown. Everybody lives in a flawlessly neat suburban house or an equally tidy little

But Will It Sell?

apartment, with matching lamps and flower prints. Everybody dresses well, except advanced alcoholics, who Don't Care.

Of the diseases that afflict Soap people with dire frequency, alcoholism and paralysis top the list. At least once a season, in each of the nine Soaps, somebody gets paralyzed either through a car accident or some traumatic shock. Psychosomatic blindness is high on the list, and it is imperative that out of every three babies born to the young women, one dies at birth. Nobody has the common cold, intestinal flu, or lumbago.

Medical and legal talk are the only two areas of serial conversation not entirely intrapersonal in nature, and I feel that if I stay by my set long enough I may become an expert in surgical procedure, diagnosis, bed care, and trial law. More time is spent in hospitals and courts, in fact, than at home, and it would appear that every American family is involved every month either with a near-fatal illness or a crucial legal case involving divorce, adoption, or murder. A brush with syndicated crime is also on the weekly agenda. I never knew how easy it was for nice folk to get involved with large-scale larceny or dope pushing, but if you believe the Soaps, that fellow your daughter is dating heads up the ring.

The dialogue in Soaps very often shows a fine ear for natural talk and differentiation of character. Living with their people as they do year in year out, the writers know them. Presumably, too, they hold no illusions about their audience; the simplest statement is spelled out for the simplest ear:

"I don't think Amy is looking well."

"What do you mean?"

Or:

"I wonder if Jim still loves her."

"What do you mean?"

At the end of each day's serial is a portentous phrase boding trouble in the next installment. Locked in a mutual gaze, the principals say:

"It may change everything . . . everything."

The Carriers

Or:

"You're determined to go through with this? . . . no matter what happens?"

"No matter what happens."

It is clear from the high level of competence in the writing, acting, and production of Soaps that the professionals involved are deliberate with their banalities, their repetitions, and their expositions. They know what they can and cannot do, a knowledge based on certain firm assumptions concerning their audience. One is that Americans do not want to see people better than themselves, although they derive comfort from seeing people worse, and worse off, than themselves. Women would react adversely to seeing a female character in a Soap who enjoyed a superior intelligence and any degree of freedom from domesticity greater than their own. If a serial woman is too smart or too gay or too sexy or too sophisticated, it can only mean that she is bad and disaster-prone. The good, simple woman in the home and in her apron, however, reaps—in the long, long tear-ridden run—the rewards.

Wealth in a Soap is usually looked upon with disfavor, unless those who own it are conspicuously civic-minded. If they should have servants (and the good ones seldom do), the only kind permissible is the warm-hearted member-of-the-family housekeeper. The woman viewer must at all times be reminded that the kitchen in which she watches the set is her natural habitat and the seal of her virtue.

As for the total exclusion of the outside world, this too is calculated, for how could people in serials talk naturally about current events without stirring the mind of the viewer out of its soothing insulation?

For this same reason, names or characteristics that might suggest a minority of race, religion, or national origin are generally excluded. A Soaper may speak with an Irish or foreign accent, but that's about it.

But Will It Sell?

The daytime serial is almost wholly devoid of humor. I can remember only one funny man in all of the nine, a detective in "Edge of Night" called Willy Bryan, and I loved him for his airy frivolity. Sarah, almost the only housewife with a sense of fun, was in the same Soap, and when a car killed her a year ago, I grieved as much as her husband. I suspect that humor would endanger the precarious balance sustained between cozy domesticity and dire catastrophe, but I also suspect that we have become as a whole a very unhumorous people, ready, perhaps, to laugh at Bob Hope or Danny Kaye but not at ourselves or at the human condition.

Certainly Soaps are designed to catch at the throat, and it is testimony again to the talents of their creators that they are able at moments to arouse emotions that are not entirely mawkish—low-keyed moments that are touching because they are believable. It is the Soaps' high drama which is preposterous, for it is crisis manufactured every day to bait and sustain attention. How else can the relentless demands of the daily serial be met than by priming the narrative pump with artifice? Twelve or twenty-two minutes a day, each group of characters must be caught in a situation which must seem to change from scene to scene but must also be prolonged over weeks. This indeed is the art of the Soap: to move without moving ahead, to protract solution almost beyond endurance, to have in readiness new crises when the last one is finally solved. At least, this is the proven formula that has sold soap.

What else has it done? Its popularity, some say, is evidence enough that it serves a real need, and that need is most often defined as the identification of home-bound viewers with others like themselves, but usually less fortunate. In the face of the horrendous problems on screen, their own diminish. The problems of their own intransigent or misguided sons and daughters pale before the dangers besetting the young on Soaps. Their own bibulous husbands may be a trial, but at least they do not vanish from the home for years on end. Their younger brothers may cheat on exams, but they are not caught in the numbers racket.

It could also be argued that the viewers are daily confirmed in the essential moralities that rule civilized conduct. Kindness, fidelity, and probity are consistently stressed, cruelty and dishonesty deplored or condemned. Sternest of all, divorce is not even a last resort. It is no resort. The dissolution of a marriage can be justified only by the outright evil of one of its partners, for incompatibility is never to be recognized as basic. A husband and wife may be irritated with each other for specific reasons on specific occasions (Janet, they argue, should—or should not—go back to Bud), but the idea that they are profoundly mismated never enters in. Correction: I do remember that some years ago there was a rather attractive man called Jim (Ellen's father), who much preferred a sad sack named Edith to his own upper-class wife, but just as he was about to get loose and marry Edie he went out sailing and was hit on the head by a boom. As I said, you can't have any fun on Soaps. Between the frying pan and the fire, there is only the solace of a cup of coffee or a kiss: rapt and premarital or tender and connubial.

I have often wondered what would happen if the Soaps moved closer to reality. If a husband were a truck driver instead of a trial lawyer, and if there was a crisis in his family not because he was in the rackets but because he was out on strike; if a mother worried about her son not because he was dating the Wrong Girl but because he had homosexual tendencies; if a young couple were in bad money trouble because they bought now and didn't pay later; if a girl were in despair because she had venereal disease.

I wonder what would happen if a family discussed race riots in the South instead of what to wear at Mary's wedding. I wonder what would happen if a Soap father decided to run for Congress.

What would happen might be the return to consciousness of the viewer; a state diametrically opposed to the desired one of disengagement from reality. The condition of fluid emotion, the mindless lull, would be pierced; and instead of that milky passivity which can best receive the sales message, the awakened mind, sniffing the danger of ideas, would harden and resist.

But, you may say, what harm is there in this respite from reality, these lachrymal secretions that wash away time and trouble? Soaps are indeed a waste of time, but there is always the argument in defense of mass entertainment that if people weren't looking at television or listening to radio they would be reading trash or playing cards or doing nothing.

The waste, to me, lies elsewhere: in the great expenditure of talent, effort, skill, imagination, and time toward such trivial ends. The writers, directors, and actors in daytime serials are too good to be doing what they are doing, which is the submission of their various arts to ulterior purposes. What they are selling is not their work but a product. And if it is a fact—and it is—that they are lucky to be employed at all, one may wonder at a society that can put its creative people to no higher use than killing time by selling detergents. All this wealth, and a wealth of care and money, goes into designing the package instead of nourishing the person. I am far less concerned over what Soaps do to the people who look at them than over what they do to the people who work in them, for this is security by erosion. I do not know how they can kid themselves that what they do has value; yet if they cannot, they do themselves equal harm.

The only harm to the five million viewers that I can think of—and this is imponderable—is the daily confirmation, as normal and desirable, of flabbiness as the human condition: sentimentality, lack of control or discipline, fuzziness of thinking, and the couch-inspired philosophy that bad people (and every Soap has them) are more to be pitied than censured—it's not their fault so much as society's. Yet society's fault is never spelt out, for society in Soaps is American and therefore fundamentally Good.

The Carriers

The pity is that there is much to be said for the serial as a form of expression. It has continuity. It has suspense. It can have infinite variety. It could lead to a greatly heightened awareness of the human condition. As a writer I can think of few more fascinating stints than to follow a nucleus of people through their days and years, freely, honestly, and with compassionate humor.

But then, you'd have to take the soap out of Soaps. And I can't see Sudso standing for that.

7: *A Time for Change*

PREFACE

WE PITY OR CONDEMN the communist peoples of the world for being bound in the chains of doctrine.

So are we. Our doctrine runs as follows:

Our Way is the Only Way. There is no acceptable alternative for a free society to capitalist democracy. Private enterprise has made us what we are, hence private enterprise must resist all restraints by, and incursions of, collectivism or socialism.

Only military power can keep us safe from aggression. Disarmament is not only impracticable but suicidal. Pacifists are fools, beatniks, or communists.

Accommodation with socialist or communist states is surrender. Reliance on the faith of socialist or communist states is folly. We alone keep faith.

Government subsidies for education and the arts lead to government control. Any government plan for health leads to socialized medicine, which is the doom of the medical profession and good medical care.

Belief in God is a prerequisite to a moral nature. Atheists are either unstable, antisocial, or dangerous. Atheism and communism are twins.

Emergent nations who chose socialist forms of government are not our friends. Authoritarian governments are our friends if they are anti-communist.

Freedom and democracy mean the final pursuit of individual goals and personal fulfillment.

These are slogans that have been successfully sold us.

Against every single one of these articles of the official American faith there are powerful arguments. How often are they permitted to be heard? Who uses them with impunity and without being accused of anti-Americanism?

They are the essence of a vital debate on our future. But who on the highest levels, where it should be argued, dare debate them? The President? The Congress? The communicators? The priests? The teachers?

They are gagged by the climate of a fear of communism so obsessive that it has succeeded in stifling all opposition and pushed a lot of ordinarily decent citizens into irrationality and hysteria.

It has diverted the great resources of the nation, material and human, from crying needs in health, education, conservation, and civil rights, towards an apparatus of armament which can neither tip the balance of power in our favor nor, in equaling that of our adversary, ensure survival.

It has concentrated our attention on an outward threat rather than an inward decay.

For the brand of anti-communism stamped on our thinking now is not just the real and justified fear of imperialist aggression from the communist world. It is not even the fear of what pious patriots like to call, redundantly, Godless atheism. It is predominantly a fear of economic loss; specifically, the restriction of private gain by collective planning. This is the nightmare that shapes the doctrine. The suppression of civil liberties is to many

A Time for Change

less a matter for horror than the curtailment of the freedom to profit.

We are frozen in this massive resistance to change; a resistance to any ideas which might, ironically, give our system the flexibility it needs to survive in a world of change.

Are you, the young, going to perpetuate this doctrine of atrophy? Or are you, for the sake of your own future and your own country, going to ask some questions and demand some answers?

If our way is the only way, why is it that civilized societies like Great Britain and the Scandinavian countries can maintain a high standard of living and their individual liberties within a partnership of capitalism and socialism? Why is the British Health Plan so provably successful? Why is the care of the young and the old in many respects far superior in Norway, Denmark, and Sweden to ours? Have those who abhor socialism ever seen at first hand what it can achieve in the way of public services?

Have those who condemn the entire Soviet system out of hand ever visited their children's nurseries and theatres, their universities, their recreation facilities? Have they seen the health and vigor of the people as a whole? If they have, dare they ask themselves whether a political system wholly repugnant to us cannot yet evolve social techniques that are in themselves valuable? Isn't the dark side of the moon joined to a white? Furthermore, is the system itself not undergoing processes of change which in time might make it more flexible? Their rigidities work against them as much as ours do aganst us, different in kind as they are.

We now live in a military-industrial state where an overwhelmingly large proportion of the tax dollar supports the technology of war. How much of this sum is really necessary for security, and precisely what security is it? Is conscription really necessary? How much of the gigantic defense establishment supports our economy; and if the answer is that the latter cannot survive without the former, what is anybody doing to change what is obviously a monstrous obstacle to any genuine approach to disarmament and peace?

If belief in God is the clue to moral behavior, why has the climate of morality in this basically Christian society sunk so low? And why is it that so many of our most productive individuals, whether they are scientists or scholars or musicians or writers or artists, are agnostics? Are there not more ways than one to attain grace of spirit?

Can the pursuit of private profit and private pleasures, unchecked, produce either a moral, a creative, or a strong society? Or has not the time come when personal, as well as national, sovereignty must be partially forfeited for the sake of a livable world for most human beings?

These are hard questions but they must be asked. Much is required of those who answer them: reason, courage, a scrupulous honesty. But more than anything else, an open mind and an open heart.

The deluge of sales talk may be closing both heart and mind to the dialogue of man.

THE HANDSOME HEART

WHEN CERTAIN WORDS go out of fashion, the qualities they describe ebb with them, or—if they still exist—no longer seem to rate high in the public favor. Noble, generous, gallant, largehearted—who is elevated now for these attributes? They have a soft and antique sound, echoing down the corridors of the past.

The hero today can be kind and amiable and easy to get on

with, but what he is applauded and venerated for is the sort of
shrewdness and competence that puts him ahead of others in the
big game. To be hardheaded is a virtue now, and idealism has
become a synonym for soft thinking. We leave the heart to the
Church, to poets, and to charity, for it seems to have small cur-
rency in the market place, of ideas as well as goods, which the
world has become.

A peculiarly unattractive phrase has been around for some
time: "Looking Out for Number One," Number One being, of
course, self. And although it issues mainly from the mouths of
movie and television crooks or delinquents in novels, it is im-
plemented every day by the fellow who cuts in front of your car
without warning, the woman who lets the swing door slap in
your face, and the salesgirl who considers your questions intru-
sions on her time. They are all Looking Out for Number One.
Whatever it was in them (if indeed they ever had it) that gave
freely to others in look or smile or care or warmth has been
atrophied: the heart, withheld, is a small, shrivelled thing.

What is, precisely, this giving, not of things, but of self? Well,
if you'd been at Agincourt you would have recognized it in Henry
the Fifth:

> "A largess universal like the sun,
> His liberal eye doth give to every one,
> Thawing cold fear, that mean and gentle all
> Behold, as may unworthiness define,
> A little touch of Harry in the night."

And had you been at the funeral of Abraham Lincoln, you
would have wept, with Walt Whitman: "And how shall I deck my
song for the large sweet soul that has gone?"

A largess universal; a large sweet soul. Even the dictionaries
and the thesauri concede that generosity is the mark of kings, for
listen to them grope their way to definition: to be generous is to
be "liberal, free, great, humane, largehearted"; "exhibiting qualities regarded as belonging to high birth . . ."; "benignant, disin-
terested, altruistic, magnanimous, chivalrous."

Lofty attributes all—in the dictionary. But what politician in his right mind would apply them to his candidate in a nominating speech at a convention? Honest, upright, God-fearing, yes; but to credit him with generosity and largeness of heart would be to undo him. Ah, yes, nice qualities, but impractical. The generous can make trouble by giving away what they should sell.

But do they? Isn't the real truth that generosity is intensely practical and that the ungenerous are the enemies of the people? What has a man or a woman or a nation lost by giving? What love, what marriage can possibly endure without generosity, without a constant exercise of the heart?

We, of all peoples in the world, have matched the freedom of our continent with the freedom of our souls and lived—until now at least—in the image of generosity. It is the first quality the rest of the world has always praised us for, and our history is blazoned with gestures of humanity and altruism that have served as models for the less fortunate and the less free. Why then should we now constrict ourselves out of fear: fear of being suckers, fear of being "soft," fear of being outraced by others?

Can we no longer afford to be generous—to give, if nothing else, the example of a rich and mighty nation *free* to give? Is it, as the "practical realists" say, "our largess universal" that has cost us our prime place in the world, or is it rather small thinking about material competition? What has happened to our "large sweet soul," once the world's beacon? That the image of business seems to have replaced it in so many places is bad business—for all.

I think it is time we reinstated the heart. The head alone can never solve the affairs of men, whether it is the division of race in our own land or the division of power on earth. Man and woman, labor and management, black and white, capitalism and socialism; between each is a no man's land where the only passport is understanding—not only in the head but in the heart—and the only safe conduct is compassion. This is in itself an act of giving; not of giving in, but of allowing the imagination to cross the borders of difference.

But it is easier—much easier—to "stand firm," not to give an inch. Our society is now so organized that we are free to stand on our rights without acknowledging those of others: the right of a bus driver to deny a passenger information; the right of a saleslady not to say "Ma'am"; the right of a stenographer not to punctuate; the right of a worker not to do a full day's work for a full day's pay; the right of a waiter not to wait; the right of a nurse not to smile; the right of a manufacturer to charge more for cheaper products; the right of a wife to demand more than her husband can afford; the right, in all cases, to take and not to give.

But the irony is that these standers-on-rights, these takers, these ungenerous souls will, in the end, be the losers. They can not, unfortunately, lose their jobs, but they can and do lose respect and affection. They lose an answering smile, a warm response, a new friend. They lose love.

For what man can live for long with an ungenerous woman? And what ungenerous man can hold his wife's love? The answer to that timeless riddle about couples, "I wonder what she sees in him—or he in her?" is easy: a magnanimous spirit.

Or, as Gerard Manley Hopkins wrote in his poem, "The Handsome Heart":

> "Mannerly-hearted! more than handsome face—
> Beauty's bearing or muse of mounting vein,
> All, in this case, bathed in high hallowing grace. . . ."

It is not easy to sustain a "high hallowing grace," but the habit of generosity can be learned and practiced. A woman can take pleasure in the pleasure lovely women take in her husband, and hold him the closer. A man can be proud of his wife's achievements and gain, rather than lose, stature by his obeisance. A generous woman can concede greater charms in another woman without resenting them or diminishing herself. A generous man can admit his errors and rue his weaknesses without denying his virtues. A generous mother can want her children to grow free of her, and yet not lose them. A generous employer can praise good work without forfeiting authority.

But Will It Sell?

Yet there are a great many people who, thinking it smart to be tough and wise to be cynical, hold to that other unattractive phrase: "Give them an inch and they'll take a mile," or "Give them a finger and they'll take your hand." I have found the opposite to be true: that you receive what you give and sometimes more than you give. I am convinced that the instances of trust repaid are far greater than those of trust abused. And if the trust is indeed abused, it may well be because of the manner given. You hear a great deal today about the lack of gratitude on the part of others for what we, as a nation, have given to them. But often our material gifts have been accompanied by moral demands: a bargain which removes the transaction from the heart to the market place. Generosity with strings is not generosity: it is a deal.

I would like to think that if we took a cardiograph of the nation's heart we would find it sound—sounder, in fact, than a dollar. But this noble organ needs a campaign for rehabilitation as the prime factor of our greatness, individual and national. Generosity of spirit is the real conqueror of space—between one country and another, one man and another, one race and another, one idea and another. The act of casting bread upon the waters is not only beautiful but rewarding. Christ knew this two thousand years ago. We might begin to remember it now.

MEMO TO A FILM
MAKER

NOTE: Earlier I spoke of the need to submerge the pursuit of private goals and forfeit a part of individual and national sovereignty in the interest of the survival—in peace and dignity—of all of us.

The United Nations is an attempt to do just this: an instrument, still far from perfect but without present alternative, for creating one world of law out of the anarchy of warring fragments.

The following parable speaks of another way, in another language. It also speaks of the artist who, of all of us, is most committed and best equipped to bring order out of chaos.

WHILE YOU'VE BEEN BUSY messing around with cameras under water, in the air, and back in B.C., you've missed a natural. I mean a picture about a big symphony orchestra: a portrait of one of the greatest human and artistic phenomena of our time. Believe me, this is no culture item for the art theaters. This is a gold mine: a hundred and five potential stories in one, and for once a way of using music legitimately and magnificently instead of dragging it in by the tail of some maestro's coat or the hair of some third-rate vocalist with a heart-throb past. What's more, this picture could pack a message that would make most of your Biblical Spectaculars look like children's colored picture books in large type—which is what they are.

I would start with the works: the whole orchestra, full screen; a hundred and four men and the conductor performing the last movement, let's say, of Brahms's First, or anything that uses the

But Will It Sell?

full potentialities of an orchestra, almost drowning the audience in sound. After a couple of minutes, I would close in on the conductor (don't have him too wild-eyed and hair-tossing—the best ones are intense but controlled) and then on his hand as he cues individual sections of the orchestra. You know how a conductor makes lifting motions toward the first violins to raise their volume, or diminishing motions, palm down, toward the brasses.

Well, follow him as he turns to the first violins on his left and then close in on the concertmaster as he plays. Let's call him Rossi; a lot of concertmasters are Italian these days, where a generation ago they were usually German. Rossi is about forty, has receding black hair, and wears glasses. He is wholly wrapped up in his playing, yet keeps a wary intermittent eye on the conductor, Lorentz—as he must. You dissolve then from the middle-aged Rossi playing at a concert to the very young Rossi winning a conservatory prize in Bologna as the prodigy hope of his region and possibly of his country. You follow his story, which is a familiar one. Rossi had great promise, Rossi wanted to be a violin virtuoso, Rossi couldn't quite make the grade in a world that turns out Rossis every month and Menuhins once in ten years. So, emigrating from Italy to the land of opportunity, he sacrifices the dream of personal fame for the security of collective employment; and it's only when a guest artist plays a violin concerto (and this can be shown in the picture) that the dream stirs and Rossi thinks bitterly: He is no better than I; he just got the breaks.

If you want to, you can bring in Rossi's wife, Maria; the girl he married at home who feels shy and uncomfortable in any worldly company. The kind of woman, the others say, who could never help a man get anywhere. If I were you, I would give a glimpse of Rossi's home life, showing him as a very ordinary man with no interests outside of his music and his food; a hard worker, a good family man and a "good fellow," in no way distinguished. And then I would switch back to him at the concert and show what music and responsibility do to enlarge a man, for here Rossi has the stature and purity of dedication.

A Time for Change

Go back to Lorentz, the conductor, and follow his cue to the flutist, Renaudel. (They are often French, the wind players, but don't ask me why.) Now Renaudel is a real heller, mad for the women and wholly unreliable, except for his playing. At the moment, he happens to be having an affair with Lorentz's wife, but Lorentz doesn't know it. You could have fun with this, especially if you could lead off from "L'Après-midi d'un Faune" and Renaudel's exquisite fluting to his activities at other times of the day.

There is really no end to these explorations into the men who make the music, these human instruments whose lives form the counterpoint to the major theme of creation. There is Wagenecht, for instance, the double-bass player. His father and grandfather were double-bass players too; it never occurred to him to do anything else. Wagenecht is married to his bull fiddle, and when the orchestra first went on tour many years ago, he used to reserve a lower for it in the train, not trusting his love to the baggage car. He is a born comic and an ardent chess player, but on the whole he prefers solitude with his large vibrating companion, who never fails him—as once a woman did.

Somewhere along the line you'll have to include Brodsky, the timpanist. Catch him first at the concert, bending tenderly over his big kettledrums, his ear to the hide as he stretches or loosens it to the proper pitch; then at his moment of triumph when the tattoo of his felt-balled sticks makes a fine thunder and he stands like Zeus. As far as his home life is concerned, I think you might make him henpecked and perhaps overcome by his wife's family, so that he can assert himself only with his drums.

Toward the end, of course, you'll have to tackle Lorentz, the conductor, for in a sense he is the key to the meaning of the picture. Here you have a highly complicated man; an artist of the first order, with a phenomenal memory and understanding of the world's music and the power and skill to project it; a politician, required and able to reconcile the demands of Brodsky and Renaudel with each other, and the demands of his board of trustees with those of Local 802; a contemplative man, secluded for hours on end with his scores; an extrovert, needing a public; a nervous, petty, irascible man, very vain; a man humble in the service of music.

Here is where we get close to the message I spoke about at the beginning. Don't look disgusted; you're the one who's always talking about making a pitcure that Means Something, that Illuminates. This is really a picture about sovereignties. Each of these hundred and four men in the symphony orchestra is an entity, with his own life, function, and power. When he plays in the orchestra, however, he submerges his sovereignty to the whole, which is music. If he did not—if he played what he wanted, when he wanted, regardless of the others and regardless of direction—there would only be chaos.

What is more, each of these men, instead of losing himself in the collective whole, finds himself. He finds himself in participating in something greater than he is: the act of creation. He has become a master of music (and essentially every member of a fine symphony orchestra must be one) in order to be the servant of music.

The same goes for the conductor. For while our Lorentz seems to be a dictator, guiding and compelling all the diverse elements and sovereignties into one whole, he is in reality as much a servant as any of his men. His power is the by-product and not the goal of his devotion. His sole and ultimate function is to bring to others what he has heard in silence: the universal speech of music, in all its magnificence.

I think that you ought to get going on this soon. Because the thing we lack most desperately now is a universal language, not to mention the humility to submerge our sovereignties in the learning of it. What we have now is an orchestra without a conductor, each man playing as he chooses; and the resultant cacophony is violent enough to shatter the windows of the world.